Follow your dre[ams]
don't stop &
press on to the [mark]
Can we see the whole view.
Amanda Bradley

...you!

Beloved Kevin,
There is no greater love
than the one you oneself —
for once you have the
good & bad & embrace
your self realization there
is only one thing left...
God Realization.
I send you continued
blessings this X-mas &
always, Love, Candace
12/25/06

BEING

BEING

TRANSFORMATION BEGINS WITH...

By
LYNN YOUNG

Master Path Publishing
Hopkins, MN

BEING, Transformation begins with ... Copyright © 2006 by Lynn Young. All rights reserved. No part of this book may be reproduced without written permission from Master Path Publishing, except by a reviewer who may quote brief passages in a review; nor may any part of this book be reproduced, stored in a retrieval system or transmitted in any form or by any means electronic, mechanical, photocopying, recording or other, without express written permission from the publisher.

The information in this book is for educational purposes only. Neither the publisher nor the author is engaged in rendering professional advice or services to the individual reader. All matters regarding physical and mental health should be supervised by a health practitioner knowledgeable in treating that particular condition. Neither the author nor the publisher shall be liable or responsible for any loss, injury, or damage allegedly arising from any information or suggestion in this book.

FIRST EDITION, 2006

Cover art by David A. Johnson
Book Design by Terri Hendrixson

Library of Congress Control Number: 2006937708
 Young, Lynn. 1957-
        BEING, Transformation begins with...: an introduction to new thought spiritualism with ""G" / Lynn Young.

          Includes glossary
          ISBN 978-1-934245-00-2
          ISBN 1-934245-00-3

     1. New Age. 2. New Thought. 3. Spiritualism. 4. God

Master Path Publishing does not participate in, endorse, or have any authority or responsibility concerning private business transactions between our authors and the public.

Published and distributed in the United States by:
 Master Path Publishing
701 Oak Park Lane, #92
Hopkins, MN 55343
952-465-8034

Printed in the United States of America

Acknowledgements

Thanks to my many clients and students for the contribution they've made to this work. Without their thirst for knowledge and their faith in "G", I would never have been inspired to put this book together. I am grateful for their help and their love and support on the journey, for without it, I would have given up many times.

I am eternally grateful to "G" for showing me the road and for dangling that 'carrot' in front of me that has kept me going when things were tough. His wisdom and guidance have helped me to find myself and transform my life, my journey. He has shown me what it is like to live in unconditional love for the first time in my life.

I wish to thank my editor, Patricia Larson, and my business partner, Terri Hendrixson, for believing in me and for the many times they have burned the midnight oil to help me meet a deadline. Their words of encouragement kept me on track.

Many thanks go to my proof-readers, Lyn Linder and Marcelle Lafleur, for their persistence and dedication to getting the job done.

Additionally, I wish to acknowledge Insiah and Gary Beckman of Edge Life Magazine for expressing their encouragement and belief in me and in "G". They helped me when I needed it the most.

I would like to thank my son, Dustin Young, for believing in me and supporting me on my journey. I love you and you have my heart felt appreciation for staying by my side when others didn't.

These acknowledgments wouldn't be complete without mentioning my family. If they hadn't been there, playing their parts in my life, I wouldn't be where I am today.

Most importantly, I wish to thank the "G" group, each one of them, whether a past or present member, for being in my life. There are too many of you to list by name, but you know who you are. Each one of you has touched a place in my heart and shared your space with me, even if only for a moment. By sharing that space, we are each changed forever.

One final word of praise and gratitude for Terri Hendrixson, my business partner. No one could be more dedicated than she is. The final word of truth is, if it hadn't been for her, this book wouldn't be.

Dedications

To Master Solomon and Master Antius,

I wish to express my gratitude to you,
For holding the faith that I can go the distance,
For speaking the truth when it needs to be spoken,
For loving me unconditionally and
Allowing me to experience the spontaneity
Of joy and happiness in the journey.

Thanks for the seat at the Council of
Masters of God Consciousness
And allowing me to participate in the journey with you.

Table of Contents

Acknowledgements	7
Foreword	15
Introduction	17
Birthright	23
Co-Creation	28
Fear	35
God's Divine Plan	37
Unconditional Love	38
Absolute Absolution	44
Birthright Channeling	58
Energy	95
Energy Channeling	106
Intention	143
What is Intention?	145
What is the Use of Intention and How Do I Command It?	146
What is the Difference Between Accountability and Responsibility?	149
What is My Connection to Intention?	150
Are There Different Intentions?	151
Intention Channeling	156

Now	179
Future – Unknown	181
Past – Familiar	182
Now – The Present	183
Now Channeling	193
God Realization	229
God Realization Channeling	243
The Journey Home	269
Glossary	273
About the Author	277

*"Now is the time
to rise up out of the darkness
of the human condition,
claim your birthright,
and embrace the light
of your spirit now."*

"G"

Foreword

It is with excitement and joy that I write these words for Lynn. It has been a long journey of fourteen years to reach a place where she is finally able to share her knowledge.

I was with her the first time she ever channeled "G". It was such an incredible experience. I was in awe that such a powerful Being of Light would come to teach us, to help draw out all the wisdom and knowledge that is stored within us.

Lynn is a wonderfully gifted and knowledgeable motivational speaker. A mystic, she gives the most incredible readings I have ever experienced. Her use of stories and life experience ensures that her teaching is never dull.

As I read through the book, I had to restrain myself from taking the time to start making notes about things to work on for myself. I shed a few tears over the young Lynn – I guess her words touched a place in my heart. Yet, even more importantly, I found my heart soaring as some of the other information lifted me up and filled me with hope and the belief that I can make these changes in my life, too. It felt like my heart had been contained in a box and someone just took the cover off, allowing it to soar up to the Light.

I sincerely hope that you are able to experience it for yourself when you read the book.

I am deeply honored to be able to offer these few words.

> P. Larson,
> Editor, Master Path Publishing

Introduction

What do I fear?
I fear knowledge for I will have no limits
To what may be given to me.

The journey always has a beginning and we all start somewhere looking for the truth of us. It may not be very obvious at first, but it is a part of the very basic drive of us being here. People tend to look for something: to fill a void, an answer to something, even a possible miracle to help out. What I know is that we, as spiritual beings having a human experience, begin to look for the answers to life's questions outside of our own personal knowing. We are taught very early on that we cannot trust what we know because we know nothing. It is very apparent when we start to ask the questions, "Why am I here?" or "What is my purpose in life?" We continue to search for evidence of our creation. "Is God* out there? Will God answer my questions? God must know." The only sure thing in the world that I know is that I

*The term "God" can be interchanged with Source, Divine Light, Allah, Jesus, Higher Power, Force, Universe, Supreme Being, I Am that I AM, Universal Energy, Infinite, Omni, Creator, Absolute, etc. It refers to whatever term you use for God. I personally use God because it is short and simple. When I reference God in this book, it is meant to encompass all of the above terms as well as other names for God not listed here.

cannot possibly have the answers. And because God is greater than me, God will have all my answers.

Men and women then look at themselves as separate from God, not as part of the Infinite. This begins the road of duality for humankind, a lost soul looking to find God. Because humanity doubts their own knowing and sees it as less than reliable, it only pushes them further from God. Mankind has taken the long arduous journey of repeating patterns of the human condition. Human condition is everything we have learned through experience, media, books, religion, schools, friends, family, etc. Human condition then becomes our beliefs. So begins the journey of separation from self and God.

I have been on a quest of finding self and God for years to find answers to my problems. It was in 1993 that my belief in God was challenged. I never thought that the experience would bring me closer to this new understanding of God. I began to find my relationship with God which I hadn't had before. I wasn't afraid of God anymore. I lost my fear of Him** and felt immense love from that experience. That experience prepared me for what happened about a year later, which is when I became a full body channel for a Being I lovingly call "G".

You may ask, "Who is "G"?" I would describe Him as an omniscient being of Divine Light who has come here to reawaken the knowledge of how to walk the master path that we have hidden from ourselves for thousands and thousands of years. He lovingly coaches us to help us uncover the God-like power we have forgotten so we can live highly effective, successful, and joyous lives. "G's"

**I use the male gender or "It" when speaking about God because of my experience with channeling. I channel God energy. It comes through as male because I am female. This is due to duality here on earth. This ensures both male and female are represented because God is neither male nor female. God is both.

warm and loving presence, as well as his gentleness, wisdom, and wit, endear him to those who meet him. He is a dynamic, eloquent spirit whose use of storytelling, diagrams and interactive discussions with the audience teach people how to live life in unconditional love and find their place of "being".

It has been through my life experiences that I have come to work with many Masters. I have learned that to obtain clarity of mind is to focus the thoughts I have. This would allow me to bring some clarity to the human condition that I had created in my life. I asked myself, "Can I see the gifts that the human condition has brought me?" The answer is yes, for I truly began to understand the level of awakening that I could feel within. That awakening was an awakening to the human "being" inside, not the human condition. Human "being" is claiming my God within.

This awakening has brought me to the next level of my own awareness. And just as I am, I believe that humankind is ready for the experience of their Birthright. We are ready to shed the human condition that has taken over our lives.

I asked the question, "Who is God to me?" In the past twenty five years, I have looked for answers and I too believed that I should never trust myself. What do I know, but nothing? I even remember being taught early on that I had a learning disability, so that must mean I was defective, and there was no way I could possibly know anything at all.

I have discovered through this journey that I now understand the level of my knowing, not with ego, but with great humility, and that what I share in this book is from the Masters of God Consciousness. I am a conduit, ready to share what I have learned and experienced. I too needed help moving forward and was lost in the height of my own human conflict within. What I hope to achieve by sharing my experiences is to bring people to the next level of their own awareness. People don't need to be told what to do, but guided to what they already know.

Birthright is the Light within us.

Energy is the fire of the infinite.

Intention is the purpose of oneness.

Now is the moment we command in our universe.

God is the power of co-creation and we are invited along. So let there be in us the God we crave.

Birthright

When the long day was over
I stood at the door of eternity
And I pondered the vastness of it all.
Was I to step through to find God
Or was it to know me?

There comes a time when we ask ourselves, who are we? When we get no answer to the question, we begin to look, to search, for evidence of our birth. Does not a person who is adopted look for the birth parents? Some of us even look for our lineage, our family history, through genealogy. This search is a physical thing and not a spiritual thing in our mind because it's easier and more natural to look at the things we can see, rather than the things we can't see. We can touch a parent or a partner or a person, but it's not so easy to touch God. This search takes us outside of us. Because of that, we begin to separate ourselves from God.

When the physical search doesn't seem to satisfy our longing for discovering the sense of who we really are, it becomes more apparent that what we really need to look for is our birthright as a spiritual being. This real search of knowing our spiritual birthright begins with the internal self not the external world we've come to know.

Birthright means everything. For so long we have seen ourselves as separate from God. But in the truth of it, is it not said that we are "made in the image and likeness of God?" Have we not heard that? Have we not been told that? So how do we separate ourselves from God? Because we believe ourselves unworthy, undeserving of this claim. As a result of this huge separation, we cannot even begin to believe a single statement like "we are made in the image and likeness of". Before we can even think about being that, we need to understand or develop a perception of the God that we're made in the image and likeness of.

What we have learned in the journey about God has been derived from our own belief systems. These standards of beliefs were created out of what we learned from our family of origin, school, religion, TV, media, books, etc.

We view God as standing there in that state of awe. We worry about whether we're good enough, whether we've done right in His eyes. We also worry about what our family and friends think of us. We do things to find some type of recognition or some sense of wanting them to be proud of us in some way. Am I good person? Did I do right?

Regardless if we are Christian, Buddhist, Jewish, Spiritualist, Atheist or some other religion, we place value on the opinions of someone else and of God. We think we know the opinion of God by the things we were taught about Him. And we worry about whether we will fill the shoes that have been placed in front of us by those belief systems. When we place people or God as some external experience or external expectation, we begin to lose what's inside of us. We lose our self perspective. We lose our self realization. That takes us out of that place of knowing God, of knowing ourselves. We can never truly fill the expectations or the needs of others because we are continually looking at ourselves as flawed and we never really truly trust what we know because what we know is limited to the level of our own awareness.

What I have learned in my journey with the Masters of God Consciousness, is that we each have a level of awareness and that level of understanding is measured by the level of our knowing. What we think is knowledge is in truth, our experience. Think about kindergartners. They have an understanding, or a learning level, of which their teacher teaches. So they are limited to the awareness level of that teacher. We would not put a small child of age 5 into an operating room to perform open heart surgery, or even put them behind the wheel of a car and expect them to know how to drive it.

We learn in stages. We have to go through those stages to build a strong foundation of knowledge so that we understand what we know here. All people, including children, go through a process of learning ABCs before they learn to spell. Then they learn to write and then they learn to read. It's all in a series of knowings. The reason I say that is because when we think about people going on a spiritual journey, we're gathering information. As we gather information in our life, we begin to evaluate what applies and what doesn't. And when something doesn't feel right or something doesn't seem to work for us, it forces us to have to go out and find the answers.

These learnings are topical learnings. They are outside of us because they answer external questions like what makes airplanes fly and why bees land on flowers. They are things that books, media, school, etc provide answers to. One comes to a point where what we learn is not enough to answer the questions inside. Religion attempts to do so, but many still walk unsatisfied because it teaches about a God outside of self that is unreachable and not about a God inside of self that is reachable.

What begins to happen in our lives is that we are absolutely everything we know from these experiences of learning, and more. We must realize that there is far more inside of us than we can connect to and use. I also started out as a kindergartner and I have become the journey of my life. I have begun to find that the indwelling, conscious God is nurturing, nourishing and fulfilling. I have found a personal relationship with Him.

Something that I heard several years ago from "G" is that, *"the moment that someone becomes aware of God within is when the universe expands."* It took me several years before I realized what "G" was here to teach me. I recognized my birthright and that I was a living spirit here in the journey.

I remember early on, I was a person looking for answers. I wasn't even sure what the questions were. I just knew I was unhappy where I was at, and I knew something needed to change. I looked for God everywhere which drove me to experience practically every known religion. I somehow believed that God was in one of those churches, synagogues, parishes, and halls.

My mother's favorite song was *Wind beneath My Wings,* by Bette Midler. It was kind of ironic that the very night my mother died, she and a very close friend were watching the movie *Beaches* on television. That movie contained her favorite song. My mother was very spiritual and she always believed that we would find the answers to the mystery of God someday. I came to have that same belief. I also believed that she would help me discover that and would give me a sign from the other side.

I remember an experience I had in one of those churches. It was in the winter of 1992, just about a year after my mother had died. A dear friend and I had decided to check out a local church, and just like my mother, I was always looking for signs or evidence of God's Truth. As we were sitting there, I had a quiet conversation with my mother and God. I asked, "Am I supposed to be here in this church? Please give me a sign." Of course my friend was unaware of my conversation and the question I had asked.

The service had been pretty uneventful and we were waiting for the minister's sermon to finish. Just then, I heard the music strike up and the music director had gotten up to the microphone. I heard him say, "We have a change in the music program. We would like to introduce the song *Wind Beneath My Wings*, by Bette Midler." I was shocked. I could not believe what I had heard. Of course, just like most people, I doubted. It was a coincidence. There was no way this could be the sign I asked for.

Later that afternoon I shared, with the friend who was with me at church, my conversation with my mother and God, asking for a sign. I asked her what she thought. "Do you think that God gave me a sign?" She sat there for a moment and said, "I think anything is possible." I still wasn't sure. I was still in that heavy place of doubt. Was I really going to find God in this journey? I went forward unsure.

The following Sunday, the same friend and I went to church again, this time to a different church, a different school of thought. Again I asked for a sign from God or my mother that I was in the right place. We sat there through the service listening to the words of encouragement. It all sounded good, but there was something missing. I wasn't sure what it was. Towards the end of the service, the music director got up and said, "There has been a change in the music program and we would like to play *Wind Beneath My Wings*, by Bette Midler." My friend and I sat looking at each other. I couldn't believe my ears. I sat there with shock and wonder. The same song, two Sundays in a row, in two different churches. How could this be and what could this mean? My friend, who sat with me, finally turned and said, "Do you think you've got the message yet?" I had. I finally knew what my mother and God had been trying to tell me. God is neither the building nor the location. God is not the external part of me, but the internal connection and wherever I am God is. Thus began my journey of discovering the indwelling God.

I suppose you're wondering what all of this means. What does this have to do with birthright? Well this has everything to do with our birthright. We must first discover what is inside of us. When we are self realized in the journey, we can truly discover the God realized self and begin to claim as a birthright our God realized life.

There have been many things that I know to be a birthright. In fact, all good things are a birthright. Co-creation, unconditional love and absolute absolution are the three major ones I will be discussing in this book.

Most of the time people do not realize just how powerful they truly are. They minimize the true power within, and the true gifts in their lives. Many parts of people's lives are either confusing or missing, because they really do not know the true potential of who they really are. What I truly hope to accomplish here is to help humankind to discover the real essence of who they are and what they are entitled to just by being born.

Co-Creation

And yet, I run from my power
Because I have no one to blame in my journey but me.
When my soul rises into awareness,
I feel the intelligence of consciousness.
My soul soars into existence and I begin to see
That the very personality that I dislike is me.
The expansiveness felt inside
A presence is the universe.

Just then a drop of water creates movement on the calm lake.
As it moves out from the center of its being
The ripple turns into the wave.
It grows larger, until it reaches the shore,
And then it understands the cycle of its life.
The wave then returns from the breaking shore to the place of its birth.

I now understand that I spent my life
Looking, searching, for love, friendship, community, everything, even God.
Then as dawn rises, I am aware
That I must return to the oneness of being.
Just like the wave returns to the single drop of water.
Today, I recognize that the radiant light is the presence of Source.
And I can only see the shine in you
For you are the reflection of me back to the God we mirror.

Creation is a thousand roads.
And we create the beauty of sailing
Through our light, and knowing
We are transformed by the very journey
We are traveling through.

One of the greatest things given to us as a birthright is the gift of co-creation. Most of us believe that we are victims of circumstance and that we have very little, if any, choice of creating in our lives. I have heard this from many clients that I have worked with. I too fell into the victim role. It was when I had reached a point of being absolutely miserable that I realized I could do one of two things. I could close myself off from my knowing, give up and continue to live in that misery or get very present in my life and change what was happening. I chose to become present in my life and do something about it.

One of the first steps to make change happen is to recognize the very present *being* and take accountability for our life. In one of my conversations with "G", he referred to there being One Rule (Law) in the Universe. I hate to use the word law, but it is what we understand, and it is the law of co-creation. When we use words, thoughts, feelings, and emotions, we are using the power of this law to create in our life. Co-creation is creating with God. The "co" in co-creation is our part in it. The "creation" part of co-creation is God's part in it.

It is simple. God loves us unconditionally and He grants us our every desire. How is He aware of that desire? Whatever **words, thoughts, feelings** and **emotions**, good or bad, we express, He fulfills them. In other words, like attracts like. This law of attraction can also be compared to the biblical term of reaping what we sow. If we put out fear, the Rule (Law) says it must grant to us our fear. If it is happiness that we project into our life, then the universe grants happiness. An earthly analogy of this could be gardening. If we plant peas in the garden, we cannot expect to grow carrots. We will get peas.

Let me explain co-creation:

- ❖ **Words**. These are the words we speak. For example, let's use the word "poor". It means nothing until we put

- ❖ **Thought** behind the word. It then sits in our mind and we start thinking and talking about that word "poor". Our mind holds that in thought and gives it meaning. How do we give words meaning? By experience. The word picks up momentum as the thought gives it substance and validity. So, the One Rule (Law) says, "Ok, I'm aware of this desire. " The thought then gets stronger until finally we start to let it go to the heart where it becomes

- ❖ **Feeling** in the heart. It is a reaction to the thought of the word. It is a knowing in the heart. When we add feeling to the thought in the heart, it picks up momentum and at this point, the One Rule (Law) says, "I must seriously look at this." After it sits in the heart, it then goes to

- ❖ **Emotion** in the solar plexus. We push all that feeling down into the stomach. We feel it in our gut. Emotion invokes from the solar plexus. That emotion creates an even stronger push and the One Rule (Law) must now act and give to us

- ❖ **Action** in our life. All that work we've been putting out there to create, it actually shows up. The One Rule (Law) has no other choice but to grant us our desire for being poor because God loves us unconditionally. God cannot live our life for us. It is our journey to walk. That is why we were given free will.

When we create, we create in our personal space only. Our personal space is as far as our arms can reach. Anything beyond our reach is God's space or God's playground. In our personal space, we tell God what and why we desire something and He figures out the when, the who and the how He will get it to us. This is our co-creation with God.

It is important to know that when we ask for what we desire, we say "for our highest good and with great ease now." If we fail to do so, we can get what we ask for, but it can be painful. For example, I had a friend whose car broke down for the hundredth time and he frustratingly said, "I need a new car now." However, he didn't say "for my highest good and with great ease now." God heard that request, along with that emotion of frustration. Therefore, He must grant the request based on that negative situation. My friend got a new car alright. But it was not how he imagined. He had been rear ended in a car accident, totaling his car. He also got injured in the accident. So the moral to this story is he got what he asked for, which was a new car. However, it was with pain and suffering. Had he asked for a new car in his highest good and with great ease, God would have granted it with ease and for his highest good. An example of that would be of another friend who won a car at a casino.

One of the greatest lessons I learned about the power of creating with thoughts, words, feelings and emotions is when I had gone to breakfast with my sister and a friend. We were sitting in a restaurant, one we attended daily, to eat breakfast. They had a breakfast special called the *Tremendous Twelve*. Of course our intention was to split the *Tremendous Twelve* between myself and my friend. The down side to that was that the cook knew us because we came in every day and always gave us more than the meal should have been. I remember sitting there and looking down at the plate.

Now you have to know that I was extremely overweight at the time and I was complaining to both my sister and my friend that there were only two ways I'd ever lose weight: one, if they wired my jaw shut so I couldn't eat, or two, if I had gastric bypass surgery. At the time, neither one was really appealing to me, but the thoughts, words, feelings and emotions around it still went out to God.

After we left the restaurant, we headed back to my friend's house. She was very upset about moving from her home of 20 years into a smaller apartment. I decided to help her and do what I could. We were sitting in the office and I noticed in the corner that there was a Nordic Track sitting there. My friend was a little lost. She wasn't really sure what to do because she was so upset about moving. So I directed things. I asked her to move the Nordic Track out to the truck, which was just outside the front door. I then picked up the computer monitor, which wasn't a small monitor. It was a 21 inch monstrosity that looked like a TV set, not a flat screen, but a big one. As a matter of fact, it was so big I couldn't see over the top of it. As I started to walk down the hallway into the living room to take it out to the truck, I was unaware that my friend had set the Nordic Track down, slightly blocking the doorway in the living room. I tripped over it and went airborne. All I heard from Spirit was, "Turn your head please." I turned my head; my hands hit the floor, saving the monitor mind you because I was concerned about breaking that. Instantly, my jaw hit the side of the monitor. To my shock and dismay I had fractured my jaw. I went to the hospital and had my jaw wired shut for six weeks.

It's interesting that I created that situation in less than an hour of speaking the words. Now you would think this saga would be over with. But you see, I didn't know about "G"'s Release Statement which erases words, thoughts, feelings and emotions that are not in my highest good. I did not realize that when we think, speak, feel or emote something, if it does not manifest immediately, it suspends around us, possibly for years, until conditions are perfect for manifestation.

You see, with my jaw wired shut, I lost 40 pounds. That was not enough in my eyes. So in January, 2006, I had gastric banding done for weight loss because I never neutralized or released the statement made about the gastric bypass way back then. In addition, I've told this story several times over the last few years as an example to others. That too helped create the need for the gastric banding procedure. I now make sure that I say "G'"s Release Statement every time I use this example of creating with thoughts, words, feelings and emotions.

Following is "G'"s Release Statement:

> *"G", anything I may have said, spoken ill, thought, felt, emoted or did that is contrary to my highest good, or anything suppressed, repressed, suspended or hanging around that is contrary to my highest good, I release it all to you now for my highest good and with great ease.*

I use this statement whenever I have not caught my **words, thoughts, feelings and emotions** that I have not been really conscious of, and I also use this statement when I am very aware of things I create that I want to uncreate. I find that this really helps me to take accountability for my creative power in this journey. I say the "G" Release Statement several times a day to help me create in a clear, productive and positive way.

I'm sure there is a curiosity as to what repressed, suppressed, suspended or hanging around means. We can suspend words, thoughts, feelings or emotions, just like I did with the gastric banding for more than three years. It was there, suppressed, until I let it go. I thought about never being able to lose weight again after my divorce. I was at my highest weight ever and it was getting difficult to get around. I felt fat; I didn't think anybody could love me. These thoughts and feelings crossed my mind numerous times and I'd let them go again.

This is but one example. Think about the words like "It's genetic; it runs in our family". Those are also all suspended around us. Eventually God then acts upon them for us and brings it into our life. This is how illness is created. We need to learn how to stop the old patterns in the mind, which I call mind's choice, and replace it with a new thought, which I call spirit's will. When we change our thought process, it changes us. This helps us begin to recognize non-productive and mundane thoughts, those things we repeat over and over again, so that we may change them.

Fear

Let's look at fear, a non-productive emotion that we commonly feel and hence, co-create with. (A non-productive emotion is any emotion that does not aid us in our journey.) Fear can be invoked by movies, roller coasters, television, books, getting injured from falling, someone saying something hurtful, losing a loved one, the unknown, death, abuse, etc. I could go on with a billion little or big fears; the list is endless.

Because our mind is the place that holds thought, we sit there thinking, "Great, now I'm thinking about fear. " What do we fear? The most common fear is fear of the unknown. But why do we fear that? Have we not woken up for years and survived the unknown every day? So I ask the question, do we need to fear the unknown? What really is the unknown? Tomorrow. Can we change tomorrow? Can we truly predict tomorrow with 100 percent accuracy? Of course not. There are a billion outcomes to choose from and we decide that outcome through our own words, thoughts, feelings and emotions.

Fear is a nonproductive emotion that resides in two areas: in our past and in our future. If we are projecting into the future or focused on the past, it is a way for us to avoid the moment, an opportunity to not see our part in creating. The past is only a library of our lives to be used at a glance. It is not a place to stay and get lost in.

If we are projecting into the future, because it is unknown to us, I call this God's playground. This is not something we can control. It causes us to miss the opportunity to be present and to fix the issue that we are creating.

Fear can push people to do some really crazy things or nothing at all. Most people base decisions on fear, like not going to the top of a mountain because they may have a fear of heights, or hurting someone out of a sense of preservation like victims of abuse who take their abuser's life to stop the abuse from happening again. A lot of times we say, "Maybe if I do this, this will happen to change the outcome." We cannot base decisions on fear because we invariably make the wrong decision when we do so.

Fear is one of those non-productive emotions that we consider a well worn path. You ask, what is the well worn path? It is the familiar road, the repeating pattern of our day to day living. Humans living their birthright understand that the familiar is everything we have been taught, the level of our own awareness. Think about a person who continually tries to change our mind about what we believe. Is this why, based on their religious beliefs, people try to save others? Religion teaches us that if we do not conform to its rule, we will not be "saved" and therefore we will burn in hell. That definitely creates fear in some, a fear of God, which invokes even more fear.

I believe that there is no wrong way to God and that everyone has their own level of awareness and understanding of that journey. Yet people can be uncomfortable with that viewpoint. Some feel their way is the only way and that because we don't all believe exactly the same way, there must be something wrong with other people's viewpoints. This is nonproductive emotion and it makes the whole burn in hell concept worse.

God's Divine Plan

I asked "G" about God's divine plan because religion teaches that God has a plan for each of us, that it's the only plan and that our plan doesn't count because we're wrong and we don't know what we're talking about. "G" lovingly said, *"God does not have a divine plan for you. This is your life; you are granted a life of free will; and you can create anything you desire. If you think that God is here and has a plan for you, you are mistaken."* "G" wants us to know that we are loved unconditionally, and this is our journey to know a loving God, not a controlling God.

I was having dinner with a few friends one night. The discussion turned to the uncomfortable topic of God. One woman in our group, I'll call her Sandy, was telling me that God had a plan for her. She indicated she had gotten pulled over for a speeding ticket one night. As a result of that speeding ticket, Sandy received a hefty fine. Her husband was unemployed at the time and money was tight, so the fine was more than they had money for. She knew she needed to find a way to get the money. A friend of hers told her about a home jewelry business. She decided to try it and became very good at it. Sandy raised enough money to cover the ticket, and she loved the work so much, it became her full time career. Now, Sandy interpreted all this as God's divine plan for her. However, she created the whole thing herself. It was her divine plan, not God's.

Earlier we talked about how words, thoughts, feelings and emotions create. Sandy has always driven fast and admitted to thinking that one day she was going to get caught. That created a fear she would get caught. And what does fear do? It attracts to us the very thing we are afraid of. Hence, she got stopped and was issued a speeding ticket. Now, she knew she needed to come up with a way to pay that ticket. And she knew she could do that and that God would take care of her. She just wasn't sure how. She attracted to her everything, not only getting that ticket, but also a way to pay for it. The gift was a full time job she desired and that helped her contribute funds to the family budget so they could pay their bills.

Unconditional Love

I once looked out into the void and I began to tremble.
I was uncertain of the unknown.
What was out there, unseen?

I once looked out there into the light.
I began to tremble.
I was again uncertain of the unknown.
What was out there, unseen?

I began to see that I was uncertain about me.
Was I strong?
Was I confident?
Was I worthy?
All are symbiant to each other.
Can I know the light without the dark?
The answer is no.
For in the light, the shadows show form.
For the God Light embraces perfection and imperfection
And this is where unconditional love is.
If the light is pure light, then I will never be a part of it.
It holds both so that when I am human I can touch God Light
And not feel the distance between us.

The horizon is everything within me.
I see hope for if God loves me in spite of myself, there is hope.
Just as I began to get quiet, I heard, "I love you. For if I am unconditional love,
It is all that I AM.
So live your life with abandon.
Love without fear.
Walk like today is all you have
And tomorrow is mine to hold for you.
Remember, eternity is but a blink and you are living it all.

People are continually looking for their interpretation of love. What does it all mean? There comes a point in a person's journey, when someone finally asks the questions. "Does God love me?" "Can I truly understand and truly feel the love of God?"

For me personally, I have experienced God's love in many ways, but like you, I too did not believe that an unconditionally loving God could be felt by humans. I believed that love came with conditions, came with certain expectations like "If I love you, you must love me back."

I understand human love. It's obtainable, touchable; it is something that I can experience. I believed that God's love was so far removed from me that I questioned its existence. I wanted desperately to find that love, a love free of conditions, free of expectation. I wanted to believe that God's love was unconditional, free of making me have to prove my worthiness. But we all have been taught that God's love does have conditions and that we must do certain things to prove ourselves, to prove our worthiness. If we didn't walk a certain way, act a certain way, do certain things, we would then prove we are unworthy, thereby believing God would hold himself back; hold his love back from us.

Now, I have felt God's love in fleeting moments, but to truly embrace the all encompassing, unconditional love of God, I have not. We have to begin to understand our worth and our worthiness in this journey. It is our birthright to feel the love of God and know that that love is free of conditions.

"G" once said, *"Just as the wave breaks over the shore, we can see the treasures that are left behind."* Maybe when we look and we see nothing, we will ask the question, "Am I ready to experience the level of love that God grants us?" Maybe we will see it all, maybe we won't. The choice is ours. If we see nothing, we believe we deserve nothing. Yet, if we truly claim our birthright, we will see it all and know we deserve it all. We will be free to experience God's unconditional love in all ways.

I had a conversation with a client. I'll call her Rachel. She was struggling with the issues of finding the kind of God that loves her even though she is a lesbian. She desperately wanted to believe that God loved her. Because she comes from a very religious background and was taught that people like her go to hell, she has kept this part of her life a secret; concealed from her family for fear that they would reject her. You see, Rachel had been taught by her family that homosexuality was a mental condition. While she could keep her relationship a secret from her family, she struggled with the fact that she could not keep it a secret from an all knowing God.

As we talked, I explained, based upon a conversation I had with "G", that being gay or homosexual is not a mental condition. How he explained it to me is that people are old souls now a days and have lived many, many lifetimes. Imagine being a soul that has incarnated as male lifetime after lifetime and all of a sudden this soul finds itself incarnating as a female. That soul only knows it desires to be with females because of all the lifetimes it remembers being male.

"G" also indicated another reason homosexuality occurs. He explained that we encounter our soulmate lifetime after lifetime after lifetime. If we are currently not in a relationship with our soulmate in this lifetime and we meet that soulmate, but the soulmate is the same gender we are, it can cause heterosexual people to become gay because the desire to be with each other is greater than the fact that they are the same gender.

He shared this with me in a conversation about an unconditionally loving God. I had asked "G", "Even though people believe different things about religion, politics, sex, work ethics, morals and even how to raise kids, does God love all people the same? Does it matter what they believe?"

He said, *"How can God be selective of who He loves if He's all love? If He's a selective God, then He wouldn't be all encompassing, all expansive, all knowing. In order to truly be omni, it means accepting all things and all possibilities without judgment, without a narrowed view."*

So, based on my conversation with "G", I believe that God loves and accepts us all for who we are. I have come to understand that God loves us at a level that most human beings do not understand because they see God with their own level of awareness. If I believe that God is judging, then I create that very thing I fear. Remember that we encounter God's love through our limited understanding of Him. We must begin to understand that God is all encompassing, all expansive, all knowing, all aware, all accepting, and all loving. His love transcends our limited understanding of God, creating for us infinite possibilities, so that when we embrace our true self, we will feel God's love for us.

I also had a client who had been in an abusive relationship and when she finally got out of that relationship, she was very shy about getting involved with other men. When she finally let someone into her life, even though the abuse was not there, it still felt like she was under scrutiny about what she ate, how she looked. Her partner would make comments about her weight. She even tried leaving the relationship at one point, but stayed because she thought that this was the best it could be and she wouldn't find better. Her role models for relationships were poor at best, and she never thought love could be unconditional. Then she met "G" and began attending his channelings on a regular basis. He began talking to the group about settling. He began to talk about how love should be without conditions, without expectation, that if we truly love someone, we love the whole of them, not part of them. We do not try to change them. We do not try to make them fit the mold of our perfect idea, for the moment we do that, we take our self out of the God equation and put our self into the human equation which then limits us. It limits love.

Most people in the journey do not realize that to feel God's love means to truly embrace their God within. If we don't look with God's eyes at someone, then they are flawed. If we don't look at the person with God's eyes then we see their imperfections. They become the mirror of what we dislike in ourselves for that's how we truly judge.

Most humans cannot see the indwelling God. They're afraid to see the God within. They only remember the God they've been taught, the external God that sits there keeping track of every mistake, of every imperfection, of every little thing that a human being has done wrong.

You see, I have come to understand that God is not like that. God looks at us with wonder. He looks at us with awe, for He sees our magnificence. He sees our perfection. He sees how incredibly wonderful we really are. And He loves us unconditionally and absolutely.

Remember the woman in the unsatisfied relationship? "G"'s words helped her to leave, not knowing what was in her future. She just knew that "G"'s words rang true for her.

She had faith that what she had heard was just for her. She knew that if she stayed in the relationship, she would have missed the opportunity of finding a truly unconditionally loving man to be in her life.

About a year and a half ago, a man walked into her life showing her all the possibilities of herself, loving her just the way she is, without changing her. She even tried to fight this love for awhile, challenging him, to see if he'd leave her. Instead, he dug in and kept loving her, letting her work through the conflict of the past because he knew that with this journey of "G", she would truly come to understand that he loves her in spite of herself.

He sees her perfect body even though she thinks she is overweight, her perfect eyes, and her perfect face even though she feels like her face is one big freckle. He sees all the perfection of her, even though she doesn't. He loves her blue green eyes that change when she wears different colors. He loves her perfect smile even though for a very long time she had teeth missing and was afraid to smile. He loves the fact that she's spiritual and is moving forward in the road to healing her heart.

So you see, it is possible to find a soulmate, lifemate, lovemate, playmate that can love us and accept us just as we are. Unconditional love comes not only from God, but also from the very people we love. Think of a world filled with people accepting each other and allowing each one to be who or what they choose, embracing each other and accepting their path.

I hold hope that we will find planet Earth emulating unconditional love. It is our birthright and we must rise up and claim it for ourselves.

Absolute Absolution

To distinguish form we must see what lies within us
And within the light.
This journey is showing us an order to its existence
And for us to understand the one presence of forgiveness.
I distance myself from God
Seeing Him as reverent and I as not worthy.
I was not ready to claim my life
For it was filled with failure.
How can I be embraced by God when I seem to lose faith?
I stood very still and waited for God's justice
And I heard, "You are forgiven."
The confusion I felt was one of uncertainly and wonder.
Could it be that I have not failed?
Was I still loved by God?
Just then a small bird flew by me.
I some how knew I was to follow it.
The path was long and hard, but I stayed the course
Until the bird led me to a beautiful garden.
It was green and lush, with vines stretching out
As though they were caressing the land.
There were tall trees that gave the appearance
Of being the watchful eyes of God.
I could see primroses, violets, daffodils, pansies, gladiolas,
Roses, and many more, as far as my eyes could see.
I was very grateful to the little bird
And thanked him for leading me here.
I heard the words from behind say, "Yes, but it was you
who stayed the journey and found your way here."
I turned around and was greeted by a beautiful light
And within the light, there she stood-a master.
She reached out her hand so I could take hold of it.
I did and we began to walk along a path.
I asked, "What is this place? It is so magnificent."

The master turned and said,
"This is the garden of absolute absolution."
I was struck with awe, that this extraordinary place
Could be a place of forgiveness.
Every time I looked up
It was more beautiful then the last time.
"How is it that every time I look at the garden
It changes, becomes more beautiful?"
She turned to me and said,
"Absolution is constant and every time someone is forgiven
The garden expands and grows
With more beautiful flowers, plants, and trees.
This is why absolute absolution is so important
To the journey of self.
One cannot find their state of being
When there is no unconditional love.
This is the place where love heals all things.
God doesn't judge man.
Is it not known that God is unconditionally loving?
And that you are created out of that love?
Yes. So to know the true light of one's spirit
Happens when one can see
Only the goodness of his or her heart.
As I stood there, I watched flower after flower,
Tree after tree, plant after plant
Become or change before my eyes.
I was so amazed at how much was changing before me.
The master then lifted her hands and said,
"Now is the time to rise up out of the darkness
Of human condition, claim your birthright
And embrace the light of your spirit now."
I was awestruck and realized that I had lost myself
In fears of imperfection and doubt.
I had gotten lost in the human conflict
And looked at myself as unworthy.
I began to see that we can never believe in forgiveness

When all we can see is nothing but failure with every turn.
The master then placed her hand on my heart and said,
"You are the child of God, made in Its image.
How can you be nothing less than perfection and light?
God is love; therefore, you are love.
When you rise up to meet the truth of you,
You will know only the true awakening
Of absolute absolution.

    I find that the journey is continually changing and evolving. We are no longer the same people in our life. What I have come to understand in my experience with absolute absolution and forgiveness is that I base true forgiveness on whether I have been forgiven by others and God.

    When we think about other people in our life, do we not want them to forgive us the moment we realize what we have done? Of course we do. It is a basic need to find and be absolved of anything that we may have done wrong, once we are aware of it. When we go forward in life, it becomes a series of events that we categorize as our life.

    I was having a conversation with my youngest son one day over lunch and we discussed how every person in our family has a different interpretation of what their life is. Even though all three of my sons lived in the same house, with the same mother and father, they all have a different story to tell, a different categorization of events. This is where the journey gets a little confusing. If each person has a different interpretation of their life or a different interpretation of the events in their life, how can God judge us? How would we know we had done anything wrong? What may be wrong in one person's eyes may be OK in another's.

    I was curious about this, so I had a conversation with "G". He said, *"God doesn't judge. He can't because then He'd be doing what He told people not to do. Also, it's because people define life differently and interpret things that happen in so many different ways. So how can God judge them all by one standard? God looks at all things as opportunities of learning and not as mistakes or failures or things to be judged. Forgiveness is really for humankind, not God. We must forgive each other. It is vital to a person's road."*

When I went to look for the definition of absolute absolution, I couldn't find anything in any dictionary or internet search. So, I went out on the internet to find a definition for "absolute" and this is what I found:

Definitions of **absolute** on the Web:

- perfect or complete or pure; "absolute loyalty"; "absolute silence"; "absolute truth"; "absolute alcohol"
- complete and without restriction or qualification; sometimes used informally as intensifiers; "absolute freedom"; "an absolute dimwit"; "a downright lie"; "out-and-out mayhem"; "an out-and-out lie"; "a rank outsider"; "got the job through sheer persistence"; "sheer stupidity"
- not limited by law; "an absolute monarch"
- expressing finality with no implication of possible change; "an absolute guarantee to respect the nation's authority"; "inability to make a conclusive refusal"
- without conditions or limitations; "a total ban"
- something that is conceived to be absolute; something that does not depend on anything else and is beyond human control; "no mortal being can influence the absolute"

Source: wordnet.princeton.edu/perl/webwn

And then I decided to look up the word "absolution". Definitions of **absolution** on the Web:

- the condition of being formally forgiven by a priest in the sacrament of penance

- the act of absolving or remitting; formal redemption as pronounced by a priest in the sacrament of penance

Source: wordnet.princeton.edu/perl/webwn

My knowing understands this interpretation and at one time I believed it. What I now understand to be the whole forgiveness thing has changed. According to "G", *"Absolute absolution is total and complete forgiveness before you've even done anything wrong. That means you are forgiven for all things, not just some things."*

If God is all knowing, he already knows the outcome, and if there are a billion outcomes to one event, He knows them all. Does God have to forgive us? Yes, because God loves us unconditionally. What does this mean? It is allowing people the room to expand, grow, learn, change, and continually find a new way. It means to allow each person to be absolutely where they need to be, knowing that the choices made and the journey picked is what each one has chosen for their highest good. It is the only way people learn. How do we judge one person when everyone is unique? How does God set one standard when every unique soul energy is different? When there are billions and billions of species in the universe? He would be limiting the possibilities of all existence, but because God is all existence and forgiveness that is all He can hold.

"G" says man doesn't realize that the soul can be young or old, but the spirit is always old. Not all souls are young, but many are. That's why they make the kinds of mistakes they do. That's why people are at different levels of understanding. It is man, the unique soul energy, that begins to create a system of events, fail-safes. It is a system within the spirit that says when I have wronged someone; I must pay the consequences for it. We feel bad and this carries through this lifetime and into the next, regardless of whether or not we believe that life is continuous and constant. Yet even the bible implies that life is eternal and constant, forever.

The younger the soul, the more mistakes made. The younger they are, the more difficult the journey because they have not yet learned the birthright of absolute absolution. They have not yet come to an understanding of being in the journey. Young souls tend to make lots of mistakes because they have not learned from the lessons of patterns. You know how you do things over and over again and finally say, "I've got it?" When this happens, it is a new level of awareness for the unique soul energy. This is the turning point of the soul. They begin to understand and they stop hurting.

Serial killers or people who have done horrible things to each other are just young souls. Think of how cruel children can be. Think about a young overweight girl getting on the bus and being ridiculed by the bully for being overweight. Most of the time, until someone truly learns the lessons of life, they really won't change.

A long time ago, parents would spank their children or whip them and then say that it was wrong to strike or hit. "G" says, *"You continually teach each other miscommunication, double standards, exceptions to the rules, "do as I say and not as I do." How could a young person not be confused by adults doing exactly the opposite of what they are told to do or not do? When children do what they see, but are told not to, they are punished for it. So you see, God has to be forgiving. He sees the error of your ways. He understands that you are all learning, even the adults who proclaim to know what they know. Is it not also taught in your bibles that you will be judged in the end, yet you are punished for judgment? Is that not exactly what I just said? It's like a double standard for God. No wonder you are confused. If that is the message that God is bringing you, then how can he judge you for he's the first to teach? I believe it says "Thou shalt not judge, lest ye be judged." Kind of confusing for mankind, isn't it?"*

I asked "G" what he thought about right and wrong and the understanding of karma. He explained, *"Do you know what "G" sees when he looks out into the yard? A tree that is green and budding beautifully and joyfully in the spring. And over the summer it continues to be in its joy and existence because it's about the Light. Light gives it life. And as summer sets and fall rises, the leaves begin to change color and fall to the ground. What God sees are the cycles of life. The very life-giving light is also the very light that allows the seasons to change. So, if a man who is walking his life in goodness and joy begins to change, and all of a sudden he is no longer the joy or the happiness that he once was and he does something unspeakable out of his sadness and hurt or the suffering he may be feeling inside, can you forsake someone like that?*

A man does not just kill. There is something lying there, deep inside of him, a suffering, a hurt, an anger, something that has driven him to the point where he is no longer able to choose good. He begins to travel the road and we know what a well worn path in the journey can do. That is why abuse, if the path is not broken or healed, will continue to live on and people will walk the same path over and over again.

I am not saying that God does not feel because It does feel. But what God holds is the true power of divine hope. God holds that energy for the highest good of all. This means that God sees goodness in all things. There is always something learned, something gained, even in the greatest sorrow and sadness. It can even bring someone to a new journey in their life. So don't dwell.

Yes, there are consequences to the actions. That's called karma. It was not created by God. Man has created it to appease his guilt. Every wrong must be righted. So man holds in himself the consequences of his life. It is through karma that he pays the price of righting the wrong whether it is going to prison for murdering someone or the consequences of coming back in the next lifetime and suffering the same fate.

When you hear the word prison, you automatically picture a dark, angry place. I'm not saying prisons are wrong. What I am saying is we need to redefine them. We currently define them as a place of punishment. In the true essence of punishment, does that not in itself breed more negativity? Does not prison define the darkness and perpetuate it further by keeping them in the dark? Does not prison breed more suffering?

The mistreatment of human beings takes that mistreated person away from the light. Think of a child locked away in a closet. It's the same thing. If you are not held with love, you will not know love. If you are mistreated in any way, this will create a person who is absent of love, absent of all the goodness. It begins to instill in them suffering, either to inflict it towards others because of their anger at how they've been treated, or at themselves because they believe that is all they deserve.

When a person steals or robs when he has nothing, it's because he has not been taught to find it. A person born in poverty breeds poverty. If you feed a man for a day, he only eats for a day. But if you teach him to fish, he eats for a lifetime. That, in itself, is the greater teacher. What this world does is generate more of the same. You put a man or woman in prison, you expect that imprisonment to correct their ways. For some it does because they are not as far removed from the light. But when you hold that place as bad, it stays bad.

That is why I say man should look to this world as a place of learning, a place of change, and that every momentum in life, when held to its highest level of love, will only create more love. What we need to do is educate, help people find the light again in their lives so they can truly heal.

How is that done? Begin by teaching them to find the God within and their birthright, letting them know that everything they are doing is creating good or bad by their words, thoughts, feelings, emotions and actions because creating is a birthright. If you teach them that they are creating something that will be repeated in another lifetime or even in this lifetime, then they will learn how to change that pattern and start to heal and correct the mistake they have made. If they are so far removed from the light that they cannot be educated to a point where they can recognize their misuse of the God energy, then keep them separate from the general population so they cannot harm others or themselves.

Not until man learns to completely change the momentum and the energy used and begins using God energy, energy in the correct form of goodness and light, can he truly release himself from karmic debt or karmic loop that he has created. It is reclaiming that birthright you have all come from. It's that place you once forgot and that you have now found again. That's what you strive for. You strive to go home. Not in a way that this life ends, but to find home in this lifetime living a God realized life.

Forgiveness starts with self. How do we get there? We begin the journey to discover what we truly understand about ourselves. I was continually bombarded with guilt because of old teachings. I knew that I was basically a good person, but I used to believe that when I eventually met with what I believed God to be, I knew I would never be considered for heaven. I truly believed that I was screwed. I have done things in my life that I would consider bad. I lied to get drugs. I lied to be loved. I lied to be accepted. I lied to be understood. I lived a lie my whole life so how could I ever be heaven bound?

One of the greatest hurdles to overcome is the worthiness of our life. We look at ourselves through the eyes of others. We base our decisions and life choices around the approval of other people. I know I did. I lived my life shrouded in one lie after another.

The earliest lie was at about age three. When I received a spanking, I remember saying, "That didn't hurt." It hurt like hell, but I wasn't going to let anyone know that. In my life, I can think of many things that I did to deny myself because of fear, wanting to do something and not doing it because it wasn't what others wanted. The opposite was also true. I did things I didn't want to do because others wanted me to. I tended to do things so that others would accept me. If I did things that people saw as bad, then I lied to cover it up. We all do it everyday of our lives. When I thought about basing my whole life around lies, I began to feel guilt, shame and judgment. I even stayed in a relationship because I didn't want to be alone. I would rather live a lie than be left without someone.

I continued to build on this journey facing only things that gave me the feeling of acceptance and belonging, I thought. That is why I felt as though I was a failure. When we begin to recognize our mistakes, it can feel overwhelming. I was there and it took me a long time to see what I had been doing. I completely lost myself in the rhymes of failure as it totally consumed my life. The more I thought I was doing the right thing, the deeper I went into my lies, because I was unaware of those lies, but the feeling of failure was still undermining my life. It was hidden from me so that I did not see it.

We are taught that it is a sin to lie. On the surface, I understood that very well. "Thou shalt not bear false witness against thy neighbor," is the ninth commandment. At some point in my journey, I did not realize just how much I was affected by the knowing of this statement. Even people that have never heard the statement are still impacted by this phrase. You ask how? Just by the fact that we've heard it was wrong to lie, that we are untrustworthy if we are dishonest. Even in movies, the person who lies is the bad person in the story, the one who gets into trouble at school or work if they tell a lie.

Even our parents teach us not to lie. I remember that as a kid, one of my parents would get a phone call and they would whisper, "If it is so and so, tell them I'm not here!" This event gave me a sense that there are different rules or levels of a lie. I began to see that lying was different for each person and was interpreted as different by each event. Or take the dangerously loaded question, "Honey, do I look fat?" We all know that this question will invoke a lie because we are trying to spare someone pain or the fact that when we are truthful the person becomes angry with our honesty.

When we think about this path, it begins to take on a whole new meaning of double standards and different rules of truth. I even thought about the white lie. What is that? What is a white lie? Well sources tell me it is when a lie is used to spare someone's feelings. To me, this says to spare a feeling means that it is okay to lie to them. Now we must understand that this confused me, and also taught me to spare feelings to be accepted. It taught me to be false, to base my life on something other than what I am. Do you see how I felt? I was so screwed up it would be impossible for me to go to heaven.

I continued to walk the journey, basing each step of the way on what I believed to be the right thing. What is the right thing? Like I said earlier, it's taken me a long time to come to this understanding about absolute absolution, in other words, forgiveness. I don't think any of us really understands the word forgiveness. It's almost too far removed from what we believe to be our birthright. Most people like me and you are continually struggling to find those answers. I want to believe that we are on the verge of change, of beginning to recognize the truth and know that God is all loving, all knowing, and all forgiving.

In a session with "G", the question about God being a forgiving God was asked. "G" replied, *"Most humans are afraid to ask this very question because they fear what they may hear - that God is judging, condemning, and wrathful. This is the God most people think of when it comes time to face their maker. It's sad that people would be afraid. What they need to understand is that unconditional love does not stand in the place of judgment, does not stand in the place of condemnation. And of course, if God is wrathful, how can he love unconditionally? The two cannot stand in the same presence. People pray for a kinder God than what they understand God to be. If God is all knowing, he knows the answers already so why would he have to judge?"*

"G" went on to say, *"I have seen many ministers and many of the ministries changing. They take the bible and interpret it into what they think God meant. In the truth of it, most written text has been so diluted, so changed, so filtered since the very beginning, that how can anyone even know the truth anymore? It's all subject to interpretation. Even this book is subject to interpretation because everyone reads, believes and knows by their own filters of life. Just like the statement that says you can have 50 people in the same room listening to one person speak and you will get 50 interpretations of what was said. Why? Because people are at different places in their life.*

Life experience, maybe even just having a good day or a bad day, can affect what you hear on a continual basis. When you can lose the emotional connection and hear things at the level of the heart, then you will truly understand the meaning because God is the heart. That's why I say a God that loves, loves always, does not look at failure, and does not look at mistakes. God looks at it as opportunities for expansion, growth and change.

You are continually learning on this road so why would God not love? Even when someone is bad are they not loved? Does not a parent love even a bad child? Yes. It is because they know they are learning something. They do not throw the baby out with the bath water just because they made a mistake. If we do not have room for forgiveness or the ability to allow someone to understand what they have done and change it, we are no better than that God we believe is judging us."

I remember a woman that had come to see "G" and in a session, she told him, "I am very upset with religion because the church I attended told me that my brother, who had committed suicide, was going to hell because he committed murder by killing himself. You know the commandment that says, "Thou shalt not kill?" "G", I do not understand. If God loves, how could He abandon him in his hour of greatest need, judge him and send him to hell? Hasn't he suffered enough already?"

"G" responded, *"You are correct. God is a loving God. You see, God knew of your brother's emotional turmoil and that he couldn't bear to be here a minute longer. Rather than judge him, God received him and held him in his arms. If God had been judging him, He would have been doing exactly what He had told everyone down here not to do. That would be that double standard we talked about earlier."*

You see, this woman was struggling because her heart told her God is loving and forgiving and it was in conflict with her mind, which contained all the crap she had been taught by religion and her family. Crap that said God judged people and threw them into hell. She chose to follow the path of truth and put an end to the conflict she was feeling. She wanted answers and she found them. And so began the journey of her following and listening to her heart.

You see, we all have a story to tell about our life's journey. I am continually discovering that the road is constantly unfolding before me. "G" tells us that we have thousands and thousands of years of knowledge hidden away inside, waiting to be discovered. I know that at some level it is exciting to know I still have the journey of enlightenment to walk. I am a co-creator with God, and we are in this together creating an amazing life. This road of my birthright begins once I let go and let the power of my words, thoughts, feelings and emotions be directed by me and not by the road of human condition.

I remember the well worn path of my old life. I can now hold to this life knowing that God loves me in spite of myself, and that I am made in the image and likeness of Him. I am beginning to see that He holds my perfection, even when I cannot see it. Every time I fall down from my own failure, He is the one who lifts me up, brushes me off, and encourages me to keep going.

Word on the street is that God holds divine hope for humankind. I say, "What a relief!"

Channeling by "G"
"Birthright"

Note: The following text is transcribed from an actual channeling by "G". The content and grammar is written as spoken by "G".

"G": Hello, this is G. I would like to take you on a journey of discovering your birthright, teaching you how to find perfect life in a life that you have chosen to be mundane in. So now we begin to learn the secrets of how to get an amazing life.

"G": Good evening.

All: Good evening "G".

"G": Welcome to this segment on birthright. Tonight we will talk about how you, as a human being walked into this life completely capable of having all abundance, all joy, all happiness. It is your birthright to be happy in this life, not to fall into the mundane of human condition. Most of the time people do not realize that you are made in image and likeness of God and if that is so, why would God give you nothing more than your birthright to be absolute in everything that you do? You see, most people don't realize that birthright means co-creation. What does that mean? That means that you co-create your life with God. The words "I AM" are very powerful words for all human beings. What "I AM" means is I am whatever follows, so, if you say the words "I am rich", you are rich; if you say the words "I am poor", then you are poor. So you see, that is one of the most powerful co-creation words you can ever have. It teaches you how to go to the next level of creating the kind of life that you all desire. Yes?

I know people say, "I have heard this before." I hear that all the time, but what you haven't learned is how to apply it in real tangible events. So we will start with the simple thing of saying words - they mean nothing. Words are simple. They mean nothing until you put an intention behind it, an energy, a thought, a feeling, an emotion. Let's say you are sitting there in your life and you are continually repeating the words "Oh, I am so broke. Oh, I have nothing. I am poor."

Think about the word broke. Yes? It means not whole because what happens when you think "I am broke?" You start to create a momentum and when you create a momentum, all of a sudden you start putting thought behind it. You worry about how you are going to pay your bills. You worry about how you are going to make ends meet. You remember last month it was tight. This month may be worse because now you are behind one month and then you are behind two months, you see? So you create energy by putting it out there.

Then just by the thought you start to have a feeling, just a little one. And it starts to build, you see, and the Universe, God, hears that. It hears the words. It knows those thoughts you have, and It says, "Well, they're thinking about it. They are starting to create a momentum here, a feeling" because fear of lack or fear of doubt creates a new kind of energy and God, the Universe says "I have to take this seriously now. They are starting to put some energy into this."

And then pretty soon that little fear that you had, because you were still kind of holding onto "maybe" but you are not getting it in time, it becomes an emotion, doesn't it? And pretty soon you are in so much fear that the Universe says, "Well, I am going to have to grant it."

Because God loves and cares for you and He cannot live your life for you, you are here to experience all that is.

You begin the journey of creating by the words you speak. God has no choice but to grant you what you have requested by your words, thoughts, feelings and emotions.

You see there is only one real law and that law says if you are afraid and in lack, in the momentum of your thoughts, the Universe says "I must give it to them." And if you are in abundance, that very same law says if you are in abundance, in the momentum of your thoughts the Universe says "I must give it to them."

So, you see, there is really not a bunch of laws to anything. There is one. That very law that you create abundance or lack in is one because you see, God grants you what you desire. It is the law of cause and effect. Think about that. You are a cause because of what you think, what you feel, the words you put out, and your emotions. And the Universe says, "I must grant it because they must want it."

God does not see counterfeit money. It just sees money. So when you put out the intention of money, good money or bad money, it does not see good or bad, it just sees the intention. Does that make sense?

The birthright to you is your co-creation in this journey with God or the Universe, however you want to call it. You see, this journey is really about making your life whatever you choose it to be. Most people, most human beings, tend to not realize the power within them, that they are truly the cause and the effect of their life. They segregate themselves and say "Well, you know, it's God's will, fate, it just is," but in the reality of it all, you, each one of you, is the creator of your life. Your life is all that is for you because it is your free will, your mind's choice and spirit's will coming together and creating.

Q: "G", I have a question. So then are you saying that everything that happens in my life is caused in some way by me? What about if I'm walking down the street and a guy is riding a bicycle and runs into me? Somehow I am in part responsible for this?

"G": Absolutely. Just like everything, maybe a moment somewhere you saw someone run into someone and you said "Oh, that's not good." You see you store that information like a big computer and you hold that information suspended in time. Time does not exist for spirit, but it does exist for you because you have created a timeline. Because you have created time, the Universe grants you time. Now you have this little thing suspended around you. At some point in your life, when you are just at the perfect moment, you let go of the thing that you feared and it happens. That is part of why I always tell students that come to see "G" that they must take accountability.

Now I am not saying that you have to worry about every thought that you have ever had your whole life. You see, in the book "Being," there is a release statement that I have given everyone. That statement is:

""G", anything I may have said, spoken ill, thought, felt, emoted, or did that is contrary to my highest good, anything suppressed, repressed, suspended, or hanging around that is contrary to my highest good, I release it all to you now for my highest good and with great ease."

Using this statement, when you become aware of something, you release it and it releases all that is suspended around you that is related to that issue. I say this because you tend to create all day long. Think about your whole day. "Life sucks." "You know, that SOB, I'm going to get him back." These things may not happen today, but they will happen some day if you don't learn to recreate the momentum that you have set into motion. The release statement that I have given you is a simple way of telling the

Universe, "I want to release anything that may not be in my highest good so that when I go down this journey, I don't have a man on a bike run me down."

You have to realize that everything is creation. Most people I hear say, "Well, when I was a child I was sexually abused. I don't remember saying I want to go down and be sexually abused." There are many factors to birthright and your journey in this life. It is about karma. You think about when you have wronged somebody in this lifetime. A time when you intentionally went and hurt someone.

I will tell you something. You are not judged by God. God does not do that. The Universe does not judge you. You are very good at doing that all by yourself. You don't need help. What you do, is, you put in a series of events like guilt, shame, doubt, fear, unworthiness, and undeserving. And all these things, because you have put them in place, cause what we call karmic condition or karmic loop. That condition or loop says, "I must pay back this debt."

Because of lifetime after lifetime after lifetime, you have created a series of outcomes in your life, have you not? Think about how many people have come into your life and you've said, "Why is this person being so mean to me?" Little do you realize that maybe in another lifetime you wronged them in some way and they are still holding onto that cellular memory, that cellular energy which is all around you. You see, your unique soul energy, that we call the soul body, this space that holds the spirit, is really the cellular memory of every experience you have ever had. Think about all the things that you may have done even in this lifetime, when you have said things or done something. You may not understand it in the moment, but down the road something comes back on you.

There is a very cute story about a little girl who we will call Suzy. You see, Suzy was very cute, but Suzy didn't understand because she was pretty young. She went into a store and stole a candy bar. Now, she knew that stealing was wrong, but her desire to have the candy bar was greater than the fear of the consequences of her actions. So what happened was that she stole the candy bar. Now Suzy grew up and became an adult. One day she was sitting in a coffee shop having coffee, actually it was tea, and she set her purse beside her. She sat there for a while with her tea, then turned away for a moment. When she turned back, all of a sudden, her PDA was gone.

Now you can imagine how very scary that would be because she didn't understand. She looked and looked but little did she realize that she had created something.

Suzy was very young at the time that she took that candy bar. The PDA might be more than the candy bar, but there was still guilt around it even though she may not truly remember the theft in the now of an adult. Over many years she was taught that stealing is bad, lying is bad. Yes? So you see, Suzy, when she turned around and looked, she did not see who took it. What she didn't know was that there are aspects of the higher self that come down.

Let's say there is you and then you meet someone who is an aspect that came down from the same higher spirit. Now you see, she didn't know it, but the young man who took the PDA off her table was really paying back the karmic debt because he was an aspect of the store owner. So you see what happened? They came from the same higher self and so the karmic debt was paid.

Q: "G", I have a question. Hearing you speak those words causes me to think back on all those mistakes that I made as a child or as a teenager. Now, walking this path, I think to myself, "Now I know better." What are the steps that I can take in my life so that I can stop myself from re-creating that karmic loop? Let's say I am Suzy. I am on this journey and before my PDA gets stolen, I have this conversation with you. My mind goes back to that moment in that store where I stole the candy bar. Can I eliminate that karmic debt and what can I do to eliminate it?

"G": Absolutely. And this is perfect because it leads into the next step - absolution or forgiveness. You see, most people don't realize they have shame, guilt, doubt, fear, unworthiness, and non-deservance. They have been told by books, bibles, religion, and family members that they're bad, bad, bad and so they carry this guilt, this shame. They carry it always with them. Absolute absolution begins to start healing the past in the sense that it does not recreate in the now in this lifetime, this very moment. When you forgive, because "G" knows that God or the Universe has put in place absolute absolution, that means you are forgiven. Even before you have done something you are forgiven by God or the Universe.

Your part of the journey is to discover self-forgiveness and realize that when you find the road to this journey of being a good person and transforming your life and becoming that spiritual being on a human quest, once you discover that and once you embrace that, you are literally changing the course of the many karmic loops that you have created. You do that by doing a self evaluation. You need to look at self, make a list of things that you can remember, and write a letter of forgiveness to yourself.

Remember things you did when you were a child and write a letter to yourself saying, "I forgive myself." You write it as though you had wronged someone and they were the one writing it to you. That starts the process. And why is that, you ask?

Because you don't need forgiveness from others. What you do need is forgiveness of self because the moment you forgive self you walk in that state of forgiveness and you are absolute absolution. When someone does something wrong, you will not hold that karmic loop because you feel you need justice. What you do is recognize that the road is about learning and it's an opportunity to expand, an opportunity to learn. You see your fellow man walking with you and you realize that they are in that same boat with you.

You must realize that when somebody does something to you, they are young souls who have limited or no awareness of absolute absolution and forgiveness. Everyone is at different levels. You have kindergarten through college and maybe you even get your doctorate, yes? Now take a young child, a kindergartener. A kindergartener only knows to the level of its awareness and to the level that the teacher teaches it. You see, they only know as much as they are willing or can take in from the teachers and the people around them.

Imagine a small child listening to its parents. We all know about lying, don't we? Lying can be kind of bad because people tell you it's bad. It is interesting because even in the movies the liar is the bad guy. Do not your mom and dad and family members say you should never lie, that you should always speak the truth? Yet the very people that say that will get a phone call and say to the child, even as they say, "never lie," they will say, "If that's so-and-so, tell them I'm not here." So what message is that sending to your children? What do you think you're teaching them?

Q: "G", that sounds like a mixed message.

"G": Absolutely. That's what you are doing. You are saying on one hand, "Do not lie because it is bad," yet you teach them something like this. People call it a white lie. That kind of confused "G" at first when he first heard it, because what is a white lie? You know, to me, a lie is a lie. Money is money. Whatever meaning you put into the intention is up to you. I cannot discern that, but a white lie, think about that. You say to the child, "you should never lie, but you can sometimes do this thing called a white lie in order to spare someone's feelings. But is that not a mixed message? Is that not confusion? And you wonder why you are walking down here being confused? Well, it starts with the very people who you trust to be truthful to you.

Think about it for your self. When you get sick, ask yourself how you created it. You call on the phone [going cough, cough], "I can't come to work today. I'm not feeling very well." And the next thing you know, you hang up the phone and say, "Come on, let's go". Do you know what the Universe hears? Sick. And all of a sudden, a few weeks later, "Oh, man, I must have gotten near something….[sneeze]." And then you have a runny nose and a sore throat and you have a cold because you told the Universe what? "I'm sick." And that's all it hears. And if you do not say to yourself, ""G", anything I may have said, spoken ill, thought, felt, emoted, or did that was contrary to my highest good; anything suppressed, repressed, suspended, or hanging around that is contrary to my highest good, I release it all to you now for my highest good and with great ease," then you have what you put out there.

Now you have to understand guilt is something that you know very well. Shame is something you know very well. Guilt is funny. Guilt is self-inflicted. You go, "Oh, I'm a bad, bad person." Shame is accepting the gifts from other people because someone says, "You bad, bad person," and you go, "Yeah, you're right." So all of a sudden you're not only carrying your guilt, but you are also carrying shame. You accepted a gift from someone else. So there you go. Your parents tell you you're bad or naughty. They do this to you and what do you do? You go through life remembering the very words, "I love you, but….."

I will tell you a story. See, the word 'but' really needs another 't' and it's the one you sit on. But when you say the word 'but', it literally cancels out the words, "I love you." "I love you, but…." means, "I don't love you, I'm judging you." "I'm putting you down and saying you're wrong." In the reality of life, can you truly, truly prevent someone from experiencing life? No. You try. You try to do it all the time, but birthright says, "I have the right to choose the journey. I have a right to the outcome of my life." That is my birthright.

Q: "G", I just want to go back and clarify something with you. You were discussing absolute absolution and how it begins with us and an old soul versus a young soul. I want clarity on the following: What you are saying to me is that when I can get to a place where I have written the letter of forgiveness to myself and seen it from my own perspective, then the next step for that forgiveness to continue is for me to recognize that I will meet people on my journey, perhaps younger souls, not necessarily younger physically than I am, they could be any age, who will do things that I could view as harmful. Therefore, to achieve mastery on this journey means for me to also forgive them.

"G": Absolutely.

Q: Then I guess that leads to my next question which is - in a world where we have been taught 'an eye for an eye' which has been ingrained into us, there are two things that I think are difficult. One is to believe that God does not judge me. And, two, that in forgiving someone, I won't become a doormat. Would you clarify for me please how I would be masterful in both of these situations?

"G": Absolutely. Part of it is, when you think about the journey and being a master on the master road, the greatest thing that you must know is that there are many gifts along the way. The greatest gift is recognizing whether or not to take it into your being. As a master on the master road, you meet someone who is not so nice, maybe a little cranky, who has some things they are angry about. This person is trying to dump it all on you. Yes? Well, what happens if you sit there and listen and listen and listen to this person and you start getting angry? Are you not accepting that anger? Are you not accepting that from them even if it has nothing to do with you? You have to realize, nobody makes you feel but you.

Now, as to the question about God judging you... Everybody knows that you have been taught by bibles and many other religious teachings that God is judging and that he will judge you in the end. But the truth of it is, God does not judge. How can he? You have to look at it from the perspective of the Universe and of all knowing. You can have fifty people in the room listening to one minister speak and you will have fifty different interpretations of the same sermon.

If God was to sit down there and say there is one thing for all and they must stand in witness of that judgment, how can God judge each person? If God is unconditional love, he would not look at you and say, "You are wrong". Even in your bibles and other texts of religion, it says God will judge you. Yet it is taught by God that you should not judge. This confuses me. This is a double standard, an oxymoron that says, "Thou shalt not judge lest ye be judged," and yet you will be judged by God. How is that?

You see, my understanding of all things is that God loves you, loves the whole of you and he understands that this journey is about lessons learned. Does a parent not love their child when they are bad? Of course they do. They realize it is a series of learning events to get mankind to the next level of the master journey. If God or the Universe is sitting up there keeping track with little tic marks or check marks, as you call them, saying, "Well, I saw that, and I saw that," I tell you, it is not good. Now, what I would like you to realize is that God does not sit there and hold your judgments or your bad road or the things that you do.

It is funny, when you look at the definition for absolution, it is to pay penance for your bad sins or the things you do wrong. Well, I think you're pretty hard on yourselves already. Do you not beat yourself up when you do something? God doesn't have to do it. You're down here doing it just fine. You beat yourself up, you know. You judge yourself, "I'm not worthy, I'm not worthy." But in reality, you are worthy. You see, you can sit back and believe that there is a judging God in heaven, or you can believe just now, in this very moment, that to love you unconditionally is to accept all parts of you.

There was a young woman who had come to me. In this journey she had been all kinds of religions, she had tried all kinds of things. The thing that led her to "G" was her inability to accept a God that would judge her brother who had committed suicide. Of course, you have to understand that she said, ""G", I have to believe in my heart that God would not forsake my brother for he was hurting and sick." And I said to her, "God loves your brother and He is not judging him. He is holding him, loving him because He knows the road here, sometimes the choice can be very difficult. And He embraces you, each and every one of you, in your moment of sorrow and sadness, joy and happiness.

So, you see, it's like never really being alone. It is always being present in all things. How could God, an unconditionally loving God, look at someone with judgment who is hurting so bad that they cannot even continue in this life and they kill themselves? Would you as parents or even as children, believe your mother would throw you to the streets or toss you away because you are bad? Of course not. They realize that this lifetime, well it was tough, and the next lifetime will be just a little bit easier because you are on the road to learning.

And that's where I get into the story about a little child, a young kindergartener. Now a kindergartener only knows as much as their teacher teaches them, like I said earlier. Would you take that child of five, stick them behind the wheel of a car and tell them to drive themselves to New Jersey? Of course not, because you know they couldn't do it. But that is how it is in this life. God looks down and says "Oh, that one is five." So, you see, He is not sitting there going, "Bad five year old, bad." No, He does not do that. He realizes…five… this is as much as that five year old knows and just like all of you He knows how much you know. How can He judge you for trying to figure it out? It's time to realize, as your birthright, that you are loved, completely, completely, completely. And that God is not separating.

Q: "G", having come from a family with a religious background, that just sounds so foreign because it wasn't what I was taught. So, for me, I hear the words yet I didn't feel that as a young boy.

"G": Think of it like this. Everybody in this room, on this planet, has a level of understanding, correct? You go through life and your family says, "This is how the rules are in this house." Yes? Churches say, "These are the rules in this religion." Yes? So, in everything, you have a level of understanding. Think of it like this.

You remember telephone, yes? You remember as a kid you would play that game and you would whisper in someone's ear and it would go all the way around the room and you waited to see if the same thing would come out. Well, if you do that with telling stories, the story is not the same when it comes to the end because each one of you has your own filters of life, your own family rules, your own religious teaching, your own family and friends that teach you these different things.

So, obviously, what you understand God to be, or this road, would only be to your level of awareness. It comes to a point where, just like the young woman whose brother had committed suicide, she was pushed to the point where she had to ask the very question of her Christian belief system or Judaism or whatever religion it may have been that she was in at the time. What someone told her, she could not accept, and so began the journey to find her own spirit.

See, man all of a sudden discovers that there is something more than what they were taught. You know, I will tell you this. Do you remember Orville and Wilbur Wright? Do you remember that? They learned how to fly. But you know what it took to do that? It took somebody telling them it couldn't be done.

Guess what? You're flying. That just tells you that when you are pushed to a point in your life where you don't accept the teachings of something that does not speak to your heart anymore, you will make a change.

I like to explain it like this. Let's say you're learning something like yoga. You are learning how to do yoga and yoga speaks to you and you are filled up with all this stuff. You practice and you become good and you get so good at it. But you know, there comes a point where all of a sudden, that is not enough. You hit that point on the wall. Let's say you are by a wall. Let's say the wall is six feet high and you are looking up at the top of that wall. You can't see over it yet. Of course, maybe you are not ready to look over the wall. Maybe you still need to fill up a little more. So you stay on that side of the wall, but something is talking in your ear. Something is calling in your heart that says, "Look over the wall. Take a chance, take a chance. See what's over the wall." And you say, "Oh, no, no. They tell me not to look, it might be bad."

All of a sudden you need more, like you've learned all that you can at that point, like a five year old that says, "Ok, I need more." And then all of a sudden you look up and you put your hands at the top of the wall, and you hike yourself up and look over and say, "Oh, there is something on the other side." Pretty soon you lower yourself back down.

But you are not brave enough yet to jump over the wall. You just know what is over there. So you start kind of peeking and watching. Now, you remember on this side of the wall is yoga, but on the other side of the wall is Qigong. One day you are saying, "Oh, I think I want to try that," and all of a sudden you say, "I'm going to do it." And you leap over the wall. So the journey begins and you learn a new thing like Qigong and it takes you to the next level.

So you see, just like all religion, there comes a point in the journey when man says, "I need to know more." It is what drives you to go further, to learn more, to reach out. It is not wrong. It just is what it is and all people are at different levels of awareness and understanding. So when you look at someone and you don't understand why they are the way they are, it is because this is what they know. Just like your family, it is what they know. And so, you start to have to look at things differently. You start to have to recognize that something is different.

Yes, you are taught, even in words. You hear the words, "It's genetic." Have you ever heard that line? Think about that being told to you. "It's genetic. You know your mother had cancer and your aunt had cancer and your grandmother had cancer." All of a sudden your little mind, who is very powerful, who is connected to all of this stuff, starts reeling inside from the very early age of a child who heard that it's genetic, that if one has it someone else is going to have it. And you accept the gift.

You go through life with fear saying, "I could get that because it's genetic." And that seed was planted in you so long ago. Let's say that now you are on the road with "G" and you say, "Oh, I know this and I am good," but you still get cancer.

Well, I will tell you the story about a young woman and this is what she said, ""G", I have come to your classes, I have done all these things that you say. Why is this happening to me?" In other words, what she was asking in her heart was, "Why would God give me this? I have been on this road and I have honored the road." What I told her was, "fearlessness." She learned in this class with "G" that part of the road, because it was planted so long ago and she did not realize it, was still asleep inside.

The difference was in how she faced the news when she found out that she had stage 4 breast cancer, a cancer that her mother, grandmother, and aunt all died from. What happened was that she found the ability to break the karmic pattern, that had been embedded from the time she was very young, by being fearless and saying, with faith, "I'm going to beat this. I have beaten it now."

And guess what? She beat it. Not because of falling into that pattern of saying, 'it runs in the family,' and accepting the gift. Yes, she did a long time ago, but she still had a choice did she not? She had a choice of following the road with her family and dying just like her mother did or changing it as she continued on and said, "I am fearless in this road. It is my birthright to be healthy and whole and complete." And once she embraced that part of her, she was able to walk past it and know that she had survived.

Q: If it's our birthright to have all these good things, why do people end up with cancer, aids, and various terminal illnesses that they just can't seem to let go of it? They seem to be stuck in that pattern and can't go on from there.

"G": Look at it like this. As I was telling you earlier, there are levels of understanding, correct? You have learned for however many years you are old, watching TV, you have heard these stories. People have cancer of the liver and they say, "Well, that's less than 10% chance of survival." "You might as well put your stuff in order because you're a goner if you've got that." You hear people say, "Well, you know, when you've got something like that, there is no hope." And that is embedded in you for a very long time.

People who come in with diseases like that, it is because of these patterns. There is not anyone I know on this planet at this point who has walked the "G" momentum or walked the God realized state of being until they reach that point of truly accepting themselves as a whole complete human being. They are few and far between because they all accept disease, illness, sickness. Yes, it is a birthright, but you have thousands and thousands and thousands of years of history that you have written down in books which you read. You accept it all as fact, not realizing that the information that you write down is just continuing a cycle of lack, a cycle of fear, a cycle of disease, a cycle of all these things. You even teach your children, when they watch TV and somebody goes, "indigestion….." All of a sudden you watch that on TV and say, "Man, I better make sure I have some of that stuff in my medicine cabinet 'cause I might need it."

Well, what happens when you tell the Universe, "I might need it?" All of a sudden you say, "Oh, man, I'm really glad I had the Ibuprofen because I have a little bit of a headache. You know, I get that a lot lately." What is that?

Well, when you have Ibuprofen sitting in your cupboard, you know what that means don't you? You're going to need it.

So, you see, I'm not telling you to go and throw out all your drugs and get rid of all your stuff because I know. I understand you. Because you have lots of years of learning, you've got a lot of years of unlearning to do. I say go to doctors, go see those people that help you, because I will tell you, when you are in full blown pain, you don't hear a word that "G" says. When you say, "Oh, my aching neck," you don't hear "G". You're just thinking, "Oh, my aching neck." You know what I like? I would rather see you get some Ibuprofen to get rid of "Oh, my aching neck," so you can hear the words. Then next time you won't even go there.

See, you have a pattern going. You have lots of patterns going and we call that human condition. We call that the mundane life. And when you fall into the mundane life, you get lost. You lose your spirit.

Q: I hear you saying a new word, mundane. What is mundane?

"G": I will explain that. What is the mundane? Well, that is that old road you keep walking over and over and over again. Have you ever noticed that when you go to work you drive the same road every day and you know there's a pothole in that road? You know all about it. Well, it never fails, you hit the pothole. And you go, "You know, I knew that. I knew that pothole was there." Then you say, "I have to avoid the pothole." And you drive along and you are in your head and you are in your mundane and you are la,la,la and, "boom," you hit that pothole again.

Now you do this a lot and you say to yourself at that point, "Why do I keep doing that? I know that pothole is there. I know that, so why do I do that?" Because with familiar, mundane things that you do over and over again, it's like you don't even realize you're there. You are so lost in human condition and day to day mundane stuff, that it is hard to see a new side, a new possibility, a new way of thinking, a new school of thought.

Now everyone out there has all kinds of ways of believing and there is no wrong way to it. The difference is recognizing when you fall into the human condition. Now, human condition is a new road, I know. What human condition means is it's family of origin, it's all those things you have heard anyone say to you.

You know, "You're just like your Uncle Herbie." Everybody knows Uncle Herbie is a drunk. You don't want to be like Uncle Herbie, but you hear that and what does that tell you? Maybe another person who hears, 'Uncle Herbie,' says, "Oh, he was so funny." And they like that and they say, "I'm glad I'm like Uncle Herbie." But maybe for you, Uncle Herbie was bad. So, you see, these are patterns.

You accept things at the level of your awareness. Remember when you were a little kid and you had a friend, your neighbor friend? The two of you walked back and forth between each other's houses until you had worn a path between them where the grass wouldn't grow? Your mom and dad threw grass seed down, but you guys just keep trampling it down like nothing. That's the well-worn path - because there is no grass there. You just keep walking, walking, walking over it. And it's interesting because you don't even realize it after while. It's just there. That's the well-worn path of the mundane.

Q: Gosh, "G", you talk about all these lifetimes and all these experiences and thoughts and feelings that we've had. We've created so much momentum in the wrong direction that it doesn't sound like there is any hope. How do we change where we are headed?

"G": Very good question. First it begins with the fact that divine hope is your birthright. Divine hope is all that is possible for you. We've talked about a lot of different things tonight. Divine hope is the part that is the spirit's knowing of your perfect self. See it there already, just waiting for you to claim it. That's birthright.

You can get into the stuff of the past and say, "You know, I'm never going to get there." Well, you say that and you're right. The Universe is never going to let you get there. It's going to keep putting a detour in, keep letting you run over potholes, let you run over the well worn path and you will just stay in those cycles. But once you claim your divine self, your birthright, your life transforms forever.

I'm not telling you that you have to take a leap and all of a sudden you're like a saint walking down the road. I know you. You know how they all say, ""G", that means I can't ever do anything again. I know you say it's possible, but my mind keeps going back to that stuff. How do I stop that?" And I say, "You know the mind can be very tricky."

We call that mind's choice. You know the committee in your head, the talk? You know how you talk to yourself. Do you ever sit there and hear that little voice in your head that says, "You know I don't even know why you're doing that. Don't even go there. You just know you're not capable of doing that." You talk yourself out of more stuff. You don't need help. So, what you have to learn to do is recognize the unfocused thoughts of the day.

Focused thought changes momentum. What it means is - you know how you have those random thoughts that run away with you that are all negative and bad? You need to say, "Stop. I recognize that my mind just ran away, but now I am calling it back. Mind, you cannot go there. Do you know why? Because I am claiming you back. I am focusing the intention and I am focusing on the good."

What is the good? Divine hope. Your perfection. What is your perfection? Every step you take with love and with the intention of learning and changing. I am not looking for someone to walk down the road and say, "Oh, I am perfect. Put me in a bubble so nothing affects me." That is not real. What is real?

A true master does not walk around and be perfect. A master walks around recognizing the imperfection, knows that it is there, goes there for three seconds, gives it what it needs, then releases it and says, "Now I am back in joy. Now I am back in the harmony and balance of my life. Now I am in divine hope and I am walking with intention to change." Does that help to clear some things up?

When you ask the question about family and you ask the question about how can we possibly change? It is practice folks. The biggest mistake that humankind does is that they forget to practice the road. Instead of falling into the chatter of the head, you need to practice putting one foot in front of the other with a focused intention of where it is going. The foot can't wander off to the left. Your foot doesn't have a mind of its own. You have the focus of where your feet go. If you know it's a pattern that you repeat over and over, you say, "'I' recognize this. Hey, God, Universe, I recognize this. Did you hear that? I know this." And what happens when you continue recognizing and focusing on a positive instead of a negative?

Q: It changes.

"G": Absolutely. It changes. Think about that. Now you know that everyone is at different levels. You know, we have many masters walking now that are here to teach mankind all kinds of things - to respect yourself, to respect others, to take responsibility for the journey. But the reality of life is that when you are living in a world that fights against the very nature you are here to learn, what happens? You lose the momentum of your birth. And when you lose the momentum of your birth, you forget the right way.

Q: What are things that we can do daily to help remind us and maintain us in a forward moving, positive momentum on this journey so that we can transform ourselves and thus our lives?

"G": I gave one just the other day to a group of healers working on some people. I said "G" momentum, or God momentum, "G" Force. That was what I first said - "G" momentum. Then I said, "G" light, God light, which would be another one. So, "God momentum, God light, God fold or "G" fold" and God Force.

The reason they use "G" is it is a shorter version of the word, it is much easier…and someone asked, "Well, why do they call you "G"? And I said "It is Good."

Let's go back to where we were. We don't want to get off track. Think about it. You use ""G" momentum" which gets you on a forward momentum in life. Yes? Using "G" light, means you are bathing yourself in the light of creation, in the light of knowing. When you do that and when you are bathed in the light of all things, you won't have to worry about it anymore. You are like in an egg, a protected egg that continually helps you through this.

The next one, if you think about this, is "G" fold or God fold. Somebody asks, "What does fold mean?" Think about when someone says, "I gave "G" fold or I gave God fold. Money, when you give 10% such as in tithing, comes back "G" fold or God fold, which means you are not telling the Universe how much to return to you. You are just giving it the momentum and saying, "I have faith."

Then you sit there with your "G" fold momentum, bathed in the light, and the next thing is the level of force,

"G" force. You know how when they put you in the machine that makes you go very fast and they talk about "G" force? Well, think of God force. How strong do you think God is? Very powerful? So, you see, what are you doing? You are literally putting yourself in the strongest, most powerful energy there can ever be. So there you go.

Then you say at the very end, "for my highest good and with great ease." The reason I tell people to say that is because a lot of times they will say, "God, I really need this help." And they go along and smash their car up. Then they say, "Oh, no, I smashed my car up." Little did they realize that just a little bit before they had been saying words like, "You know, I really have a hard time seeing behind me and when I back up I'm really worried I can't see what's back there." All of a sudden, what happens? They back into a car and crunch the fender. And when that happens they don't realize that their thoughts had already put it in motion. So that's why I say this.

You have to be very careful what you say. Like the person who says, "I want a new car. God I want a new car." Well, that's part of co-creation. Co-creation says, "Tell me 'what'. Tell me what you desire, give me the details of 'what' and 'why'. The rest - 'how' and 'when' is not your playground. That's God's playground, God's work. You see, right there, the only thing you are responsible for is the 'what' and the 'why.' God is responsible for delivering the rest.

Now, remember the story about the person who said, "God I need a new car," but didn't say with highest good and great ease? Well, that person got into a car accident. They got a new car, but they had all the other stuff that goes with it, neck and back pain you know. You still have to be responsible for the words you speak. You have to remember you are a co-creator. Part of it is that you have to recognize there is always an outcome, always something that happens.

You have to focus it for highest good and with great ease. You see, that is vital. That is vital.

When you stand there say, "I desire a new car, "G", and I desire the money to cover it too." I have people say, "I desire a new car, "G"," but then they forgot to ask for the money to cover it. Then they say "Ahhhh, I can't do it." See, highest good and with great ease. Be specific. I desire details. God desires details. That is what it is all about.

Q: "G", why does God want details?

"G": Because he wants to make sure that He is giving you exactly what you want. Most of the time, you are very ambiguous and say, "I want this guy," or, "I want a guy in my life," or "I want a woman in my life." When you don't get specific, all of a sudden that guy, if you didn't say great guy or great girl, all of a sudden yeah, you get a guy all right, or you get a girl all right. But maybe that person doesn't hold jobs too well and all of a sudden you are supporting them. So, details. "I desire a guy or a girl that is financially sound and I desire ….."

You can get very specific. Make a list. I always say lists are good, but remember to let them go because when you hold onto your lists and you don't let it go, you're like a little kid.

You know about the little kid with a toy that is broken and they go to their grandpa and say, "Grandpa my toy broke and I need your help. You know the kind of toy that when you pull them the little bear goes ding, ding, ding as it is going along. Well, the little boy's bear was going ding… when it was supposed to be going ding, ding. Do you see that? And so the little boy goes to the grandpa and says "Grandpa, it only dings once and it needs to ding twice. I don't understand. It's not working. Will you fix it?" And grandpa says, "Certainly."

So, the grandpa takes the toy and is working on it while the little boy is still holding on to the string…. waiting…. waiting, not letting go of the string…..waiting. You have to understand something that is very funny about this. The little boy didn't let go of the string and finally yanked it back and said, "Grandpa, you didn't fix it!" And he said, "How could I? You wouldn't let go."

So, think about that when you are going forward in your life and are going, "God, I need to get this fixed, right here. I've got hold of it. When are you going to fix it?"

What happens when you have an e-mail that you wrote that you didn't send? You didn't let it go. It sat in your inbox, in your……I think they call it a draft file or that place where it's still sitting there waiting. And you are waiting for an answer, and you are waiting. It's funny, they do that a lot. They write an e-mail and forget to do the 'send'. I think that's what they do. They push on the button. "G" is not very techno so you have to bear with me on that. Think about that e-mail that you didn't send and why you're mad because someone didn't respond back - and they say, "Well I never got it." "You never sent it." That's the same analogy. You have to send it and let it go. You can't leave it in draft form. It doesn't work.

Those are the things that help you. You have to meditate. You need to put yourself into that place of 'state of being'. It's vital to the road for you that if you want to have it all, then you need to be very specific about having it all.

It's interesting, because what I did with a group of people was, I gave them a journal and I said, "Here is the book of creation." Now you can imagine what kind of power that has. People have that book that I gave them and they write in it because it's a journal. When they write all the things they ever wanted and just let it go, what do you think is going to happen? It's going to create. Correct?

Well, I have had many, many students say, "Oh, my

God, "G", my life is changing. It's just transforming. I don't believe it. I don't know how this is happening." "G" goes, "I do." Because what you are doing is putting out there the intention of what you want.

But part of this road about birthright, co-creation, absolute absolution, is that God loves you. You don't have to worry about all these things anymore because you are walking the road with a new idea, with a new vision for your life, knowing that when you are walking, you know that everything you say and do is a creation of life.

If you are not happy, if you do not like your life, change it. Do not sit in the wallows of human condition, and mundane, and go ""G", my life sucks." God goes, "Ok, you got suck." Why do you do that? Because it's familiar, a well worn path, mundane thoughts, human condition, things you have been learning. You have a whole book on that, many books on that. Actually, I believe there are libraries so big, they are still building walls on them.

What I hope to achieve with this book, with the help of Lynn, in getting this point across to the world, is to let people know that from the very moment in life when a child is born…if you can imagine raising a child in the knowing of it's birthright, could you stop that child? They would be fearless. They would be independent. They would be sacred in the journey and they would know unconditional love because they would know that everything they do, every part of their life, is making a difference.

You see, you are loved unconditionally. So what, you made a mistake. Well, so does everyone. I can tell you this. You know what they say, "If you do this you will go to heaven." Do you know how many people really truly have a difficult time believing that they are worthy and deserving of being in heaven? Most people do not believe it because they have lied, they have cheated, they have stolen, they have wronged someone in some way, and they have wronged themselves.

They sit back and say, "How do I do this, "G"?" Well, the truth of the matter is, in this journey, you are loved unconditionally. God knows that you are here learning the most magnificent, amazing journey. We can't slight you for that. You can't be put down for figuring it out. The greatest loss is in not trying. The greatest loss in your life is not recognizing that just once you can stand up when you are unhappy, turn around and you can see the day differently.

When you walk out the door in the morning instead of taking that same road to work that you have driven every day for fifteen years or five years, take a different route. Go a different way. Do you know why? Because you might realize a sunrise is different from a different angle or that a lake or a pond was there. You saw ducks coming out of the water and you saw the new babies. This is all new instead of falling into the routine of a mundane life, same stuff different day. I like to say this….and I know people will get offended but that's ok….same shit, different day. The reality of the road is that when you don't look at your life and you are just mindlessly walking your life, you miss it.

It was interesting. One day, there were several people sitting and waiting for a class when there was a beautiful rainbow reaching from one end of the sky to the other, not a half rainbow, not a quarter rainbow, but a full rainbow. And, of course, do you know what God did? He decided to really make it great and he doubled it. Now think about if everyone had been stuck in a rut. Guess what would have happened? They would have missed the double rainbow.

A lot of people that saw that rainbow went to "G"'s class and said, "Oh, we saw a double rainbow," and others said, "I didn't see that. When was it?"

That's what I'm talking about. When you are so consumed by the human condition and old patterns, you lose the magnificence of the day, the brilliance of the light. Sit in your awe. Watch a sunset. See the rays of light, like God's fingers reaching out to embrace. Sit and watch instead of rushing by in your life, driving in your car, racing to wherever you need to be. If you rush through your day, you miss an amazing life.

Q: "G", what about the constraints of life, whether they be time, money, or all these things that we are caught up in here?

"G": I will tell you this. Remember I said you are a co-creator? If you have the power to create your whole life, can you not create the momentum of money that you need? God is very creative. He has the whole of the universe to figure it out. You have your very limited, very small part of your knowing. Correct? So, why limit God? Why take the power out of his hands? Why not co-create by saying to yourself, "time does not exist," "I am always in the perfect place in perfect time."

When you go forward in that, it's amazing how you don't need to wake up to an alarm clock. You will wake up because it is supposed to be, and when you do, you will wake up and say, "Wow, this is good. I woke up earlier. That is good." And then you get out of bed and you say "This is good." And all of a sudden you look out and say "Oh, my God, it's a sunrise. I haven't done this in a long time." And you get up and watch the sunrise. You look down and say, "You know, I'm not going to worry about time. I'm just going to get ready for wherever my day will lead me."

Now if you have a job, obviously I'm not going to tell you not to go to work because that's crazy. But create your job. You know, I know you people here. Humankind says, "Oh, yeah, job. How do you get out of a mundane job?"

Well, you know what? No job is mundane unless you are consumed by the mundane. When I teach people how to find themselves, to find their road, to find their journey, their job all of a sudden changes. Either it becomes the perfect job or the perfect job comes to them.

I have a student who right now is a doctor. She is in the last year of her residency. And what's very interesting, is that she talks to me very much. She says, ""G", I really need help today. Thank you for that. My mind kind of went somewhere and I'm really sorry about that. I just wanted to let you know that."

Now, I have to tell you, she has talked to me her whole life. See, she is an only child so she had me as her friend, you know. She would say, "Oh, this is my friend." And she would talk to me and she would say, "Oh, here I am, isn't this nice?" Or she would sit there and say, "Oh, I am in a bad place."

Now in this journey when she has a conversation with "G" and she talks, she says, "You know, "G", this patient came in today and I'm a little concerned so you know what I'm going to do? I'm going to turn him over to you. I think I'm going to let this be whatever it needs to be because I don't want to drive their car. I will do everything it takes to save them, to help them, whatever their road may be. If it is meant for them to be, let it be, "G"." And she says, "for their highest good and with great ease and my highest good and with great ease." And it's amazing.

Q: I heard you say, 'driving my car', or 'driving their car'. What to you mean by that?

"G": That's a very good question. This body, what we call unique soul energy, is a product of your spirit. Now your spirit has to have something to live in down here because spirit, when not in physical form, is like little orbs floating around. The only time you catch them is maybe on a picture or maybe you might see them if you're psychic or intuitive or whatever. Some people say, "Oh, man, the room is full of orbs today."

The spirit needs to have a place and this body is the vehicle or car of the spirit. So, when I say 'driving your car', I mean you should drive your car because you should be always in your driver's seat. Have you ever let someone else drive your car? Have you ever done that? I will tell you what happens when someone else drives your car and they are not in a good place or you are not in a good place. They back into someone else's car and all of a sudden the back car connects to the front car and suddenly they're both crunched. That's kind of interesting because there is a message in all this. That message is that you need to stay present in your car and you need to realize you are responsible for your car, this vessel. This body is a vessel.

Your real physical car, you know, the one you drive to work in, you need to look at that because it is really a real representation of you. So, if you have a lot of crap in your car, a lot of stuff lying around in your car, clean it up folks. That means this car (body) has a lot of crap in it. You wonder why your back hurts. Well, have you looked in your back seat? Wow. There is a lot of stuff in there. No wonder your back hurts.

What happens when you neglect the car you drive around in? The vessel of your spirit needs to get into a car to get to work. So think about that - what happens if you neglect it? It breaks down, starts to have problems. You are driving around and doing good and all of a sudden it goes [cough, cough, cough] and you go, "Oh, oh, my car is coughing. Why is my car coughing? Must be bad gas." Think about that.

One of the interesting things is, when you think about what is happening in your life and your car coughs, did you accept a gift? Yeah, you did. So, you are letting someone else drive your car. You know how you get to work and somebody next to you is going cough, cough, cough, achoo? And you go, "Oh, oh. She has a cold." You get out the antiseptic, the anti-germ stuff that you put on your hands, and you don't want to touch anything that they touched because you are worried that you're going to catch it. Right? All of a sudden, guess what happens? Cough, cough, cough, achoo. Guess who's got it? You do. So I'll tell you something, when somebody's coughing you say, "I got a God shot, I'm immune. I don't have to worry about anything. I'm good." I will tell you, it works because you have a choice….get sick, don't get sick. I had somebody do this to me recently and what was interesting about it was that she said, "You know, I've been saying over and over again that I'm "G" immune and I went along and I still got sick. I was doing the '"G" in motion'. I was doing the whole "God momentum" thing and "G" light, "G" fold, "G" force. Why did I still get sick?"

You have to understand something. What happens when you neglect yourself? You get sick. Why? Because old patterns say when you are run down, burning the candle at both ends, running yourself ragged, you get sick. Somebody says to you, "your butt is dragging on the floor," you start playing the old tapes and your body says, "Oh, this is the time to get sick," and voila! All of a sudden, you're sick.

So, remember the momentum is that you drive your own car, but don't accept the gifts from other people. You know how you get a passenger in the car who's a side seat driver that says, "Look out. Oh, my God," and they're trying to hit the brake and there is no brake there? Did you ever do that? And you ask, "What is your problem? I am under control here." Well, you know what? A lot of people have a really difficult time being in the front seat while you're driving.

Have you ever seen that back seat driver that says, "You know, you really need to slow down" or "Why aren't you driving fast enough?" "Are we there yet?" Have you heard that? That is funny because you're sitting there thinking, "I would like to open the door and just push them out but I know that's not very nice. So I won't do that because I'm a master on a master road and I'm all love." You start putting a big old love bubble around them and they quiet down and actually kind of get into it.

It was really funny. I had a person who used to be a really bad back seat driver. And, you know, the person who drove the car never understood why every time that person got in the car they would pass out. Well, the reason that happened was that they kept going, "Oh, my God, "G" can you do something about this?" They would always be jerking and slamming on the brake and grabbing the dash and it would scare the driver and she would ask, "What are you doing? Stop that. You scare me." You know, that kind of thing.

Well, she said, "G" for our highest good and great ease, can you help me with this? I'm trying to be all masterful here and I want to make sure I get from here to there in a good way. So, I'm turning this over to you, "G"." And all of a sudden the person went, clunk, head back, snoring like crazy, sleeping like a baby. And they get to the location and slow the car and the person wakes up just like a snap. And they say, "We're here?" "Thanks, "G", this is good."

Q: "G", is this another example of what you have referred to as co-creation? You have talked about birthright and a lot of these examples of things that we had said and done and accepted whether it's been sickness, a disease, cancer, and all kinds of stuff and that it is birthright and human condition. How does this all come together?

"G": Think of it like this. When you are in birthright, you don't have human condition because human condition is falling into that side seat driver, that back seat driver, that person driving your car. You're accepting a negative gift. That is human condition, that's not birthright. Well, it is the negative side of birthright.

What you have to start doing in your birthright is to take charge of it instead of falling into what is called 'out of control'. Have you ever seen a top, you know the kind where you push them up and down and they spin really fast? Well, I bet everybody in this room and on this planet knows what spinning is. Everyone in this room knows what chaos is - it's familiar. What you do is, you keep creating spins. You keep creating chaos. And that is human condition because it's familiar, a well worn path, something you know.

The difference is, a master, when they claim their birthright, no longer falls victim to human condition. They no longer are lost in their life. They all of a sudden rise up.

You know how, in an ocean, people do that whole surfing thing? Have you ever been on a surfboard and a wave comes in and they are all going really fast to catch it? They want to get on top of the wave? They want to catch the ride? Man, if that wave runs you down, you're sucked right underneath, aren't you? But if you can stay just right, in the right part of it, you have the best ride of your life. Stay on top of the wave folks. Don't get caught in the undertow of life. Don't get lost way down deep because the undertow, human condition, says you're not worthy; you're not forgiven; you're judged, you're not loved. Mankind only knows love to a certain level. Do you know what it understands? Love with conditions. "If I love you, you have to love me back."

Unconditional love is love that is sent out without any conditions. Its only intention is for the highest good for that person, whatever that may be. You accept whatever road they choose, whatever part of their life. Driving someone else's car is saying, "If I love you, <u>you must love me back</u>." That is driving someone else's car. That is saying that you must do what I say.

How many of you hate it if someone tells you, you have to do something? Everybody in the room, I see. So, you have a whole room full of people and you all hate it when somebody tells you that have to do something. Aren't you like a little kid? You go, "I'm fighting this one. I'm not doing it." And all of a sudden you become a little rebellious. They say, "Oh, the rebel." Well, rebel, don't go into that, don't fall into that. Recognize that every part of your life is a co-creation with God and that you can be everything. If you make a mistake, correct it.

Absolute absolution, in the terms of what man understands that to be, is really 'you are forgiven before you have done it.' Somebody asks, "How can that be?" I will tell you how it can be. If God knows every possibility out there, if there are billion, billion, billion, billion, trillion, gazillion, I think they say, outcomes, and God knows them all, he would have to be forgiving. Do you know why? Because an unconditionally loving God knows that the choice made that day had many variables that caused the person to choose what they did.

Think about what you do in life. You're going along, doing pretty good, and all of a sudden you make a choice, well, not such a good choice. Let's say you're going down the road and you choose asthma. You know what that is. It is where you kind of suffocate. You can't get air out. You can get air in but you can't get air out most of the time. Here you are in life and you accept that life and you say, "Here I am. I'm sick. How do I get past this?" Now, if God is not forgiving, if God is not unconditional love, you could not change the outcome of your life. You would not have a choice in it.

You see, when people hear the word, 'sin', they go, "Oh, bad." But do you know what sin really means? A mistake. It really means to slip or slide, in the Aramaic version, anyway. That's the interpretation of it. And to slip or slide, well, everybody falls down. Everyone makes a mistake because, how else do you learn? How do you truly learn? By making mistakes and saying, "Ow, that hurt. I'm not doing that again." How could God get mad at you for learning to get to where you need to be? He can't.

Forgiveness says, "You are forgiven before it is done," because God knows that the true intention of your spirit, the true intention of your life, is to be better, to work harder, to go to the next level.

I know there are people out there that have done some pretty bad things....rape, murder. Well, there is that thing called karma again. You know, that whole thing about karma? Think about if you were a soldier in Nazi Germany and you were working in the concentration camp of Auschwitz. You happened to pick that lifetime and you happened to be a German who is now forced to enter the German army, and then you are forced to do something. You see? All of a sudden you get into the whirlwind of killing people. Yes? Of course, because of the thousands and thousands of years of teachings of 'an eye for an eye,' right or wrong - well, think about that teaching.

In that teaching you begin to do exactly what you were taught. So, in your fail-safe, you create this loop of karma that says, "I killed these people, now I have to pay penance. I have to do these things in order to right the wrong." All of a sudden you have people that do that and you get killed by this person or someone you love, or something happens. You don't know what may have happened in a past life. You may not know what contract or karmic loop they have chosen that they must correct.

Q: "G", are you saying that when terrible things happen on this planet, for example Rwanda, or mud slides, or tsunamis, that the people who are affected by them had a role to play out in this lifetime for a lesson that either they needed to learn or they needed to teach others?

"G": Absolutely. Think about 9/11 and how horrible that was for everyone here in the United States. You think about Rwanda and the massacres that happened in that country. Or think about that tsunami that came in and literally wiped out many, many people and killed them. You have to know there are some things in life that come to help awaken the planet to what it has done. Sometimes people choose the road to say, "I have done something wrong" and in order to appease that, they have decided at some point before they came down that they will be the one that will die in a disaster or in anything. And in that, it is their penance at that point. Do you see what I am saying? To appease what they felt was wrong.

That is why I am telling you, if you are in this life and you go forward now, in forgiveness, always forgiving all people, never holding onto a judgment or criticism, looking at everyone with unconditional love, you will walk karma free in this lifetime. There is good karma, too, so what you do is replace bad karma with good karma, And from this point forward you will always be in that place. You see? That's how it starts. That is the original birthright, to always walk in absolute good karma. Wouldn't that be good? Very good. Have you not walked this road and felt the amazing life? It is time to start to claim the life you were born to have and be.

All: Thank you "G".

"G": You're very welcome. Thank you.

Energy

I have forgotten every detail of the moment,
Yet God is continually flowing toward me.
I know as long as I am on the path,
I will continue to move toward consciousness.
I was awakened to this path and now I am a guest here.
Visiting only for a lifetime, then I return to the universe.
I report to the mass what I have discovered.
I see the uniqueness of my own experience.
No other will have lived as I have.
So on this journey, I am the scout,
I am the pioneer, I am the trailblazer, I am the pilgrim,
I am the entrepreneur,
I am the courageous first; I am the adventurer
For there is only me that lives this life.
No one can do it just like me.
So look out at your life.
See the road you have cut that is only you.
You, too, go forward as an explorer
Seeing this life as only you can see it.
Whatever journey you choose is but the simple words –
I AM the wind that blows.
I AM the rays that shine.
I AM the song that birds sing.
I AM the wave that breaks over the shore.
I AM the candle that dispels the darkness.
I AM the calm in the chaos.

I AM the oneness in the being.
What is this power I AM?
The God Light in all.
So who I AM is a mirror of you.
I see no life.
I only experience life for the soul is of consciousness
And the world is the reflection of us.
To be outside your life is to be outside God's Light.
When I heard the words,
"Fall into your master self and expand,"
I did not stop to pick at my shortcomings.
I embraced my uniqueness.
The illumination of my spirit began
And I stood in awe.
I now understand the power of wisdom.

In this part of the book I desire to bring clarity to what is Energy: God/Source/Infinite energy, Divine Spirit energy, mind energy, emotional energy, intuitive energy and the use of unique soul energy.

To begin, let us look at the dictionary definition of energy.

Definitions of **energy** on the Web:

- ❖ (physics) the capacity of a physical system to do work; the units of energy are joules or ergs; "energy can take a wide variety of forms"
- ❖ forceful exertion; "he plays tennis with great energy"; "he's full of zip"
- ❖ enterprising or ambitious drive; "Europeans often laugh at American energy"
- ❖ an imaginative lively style (especially style of writing); "his writing conveys great energy"; "a remarkable muscularity of style"
- ❖ a healthy capacity for vigorous activity; "jogging works off my excess energy"; "he seemed full of vim and vigor"

- Department of Energy: the federal department responsible for maintaining a national energy policy of the United States; created in 1977

Source: wordnet.princeton.edu/perl/webwn

- Energy is a fundamental quantity that every physical system possesses; it allows us to predict how much work the system could be made to do, or how much heat it can produce or absorb. In the past, energy was discussed in terms of easily observable effects it has on the properties of objects or changes in state of various systems. Basically, if something changes, some sort of energy was involved in that change.

Source: en.wikipedia.org/wiki/Energy

Most people understand energy to be in many forms: electrical, vibrational, light, sound. This list can go on and on. Everything is a form of energy. It's just the level of the intensity of energy. Think of human and animal life or all living energy as being a very high vibration. Yet it is still dense when we compare it to spirit. Inanimate objects are even denser. The true essence of energy is malleable. It can be harnessed into everything because it is energy.

Nature itself creates energy. The wind is a good example. We use it to power electricity in some places of the world. If anyone has ever seen a waterfall, one can see that water has tremendous energy. That is why dams exist. We use water to generate electricity.

Birds have a full understanding of energy. They use the energy of movement as a way of getting where they need to be. They move the energy under their wings to fly. They also move their wings and that's a form of energy.

The sun has great energy. It's a light that shines down. Every part of this planet is based on photosynthesis because we need to have that. It is a basic desire in us to have it. That's why people suffer from seasonal affective disorder. The sun is a physical external thing. Why not find that same energy within our selves? People say they need the sun and the light. We do because that is a part of how this planet is set up. But we can thrive; we can make a decision or choice in how we are affected. That's use of energy. Making a choice is use of energy because it's all energy. When you make a decision you're using energy. When we're not making a decision we're using energy. So why not take hold of it and make the best use of it?

Breathing air in is energy. Breathing out is energy. Air is energy. Sound is energy. You listen to the birds sing. That's energy.

Even money has energy. It must be honored and treated with respect, used responsibly in order for it to grow into and remain abundant.

"G" sees words, thoughts, feelings and emotions as energy. Those energies the universe understands because it is the creative energy. When we take the ability of co-creation energy with the true essence of God energy, shazaam. Creation happens. If we take the "co", which is self in co-creation, and we harness that very energy to what we want and why we want it, the "creation" in co-creation grants us the desired results.

Man is always trying to contain energy, harness it, use it, do whatever it takes to get something from it. And yet the very energy of self they don't use. Why is that?

"G" says, *"The moment a person comes into physical form, there is a disconnection of knowing that happens. When that happens, a person begins to forget every detail of them. It's like they have to come back after a long sleep to awaken to what is truly conscious energy. When that happens, a metamorphosis begins and man begins to understand a little bit more each day that they are moving towards something. What that is, is an awakening to discover the true spirit's will energy that creates from God energy. Why does man forget? Because most of the time they get confronted with the day-to-day things of life and they forget to command that very energy that can help them."*

When I asked "G" what causes that awakening, he replied, *"The dissatisfaction of life. You can't stop evolution. If you try to stop evolution, you're slowing your own process. In fact you can't stop it, but you can slow it down. Humankind has done that for a very long time. It has slowed down to a snail's crawl. You have to rise up again. You don't realize how much power you have, the amazing gifts that you have within. That is difficult for "G" sometimes. He knows what He knows, yet you deny it. He tells you about it and you still deny it. I truly believe you are on the verge of pushing yourselves to your potential instead of minimizing it. That's why I say you must live your joy; trust in the momentum of your life. When you do that, you feel happy. You don't have to look at your life with regret. Look at the energy of your life as a true answer, a true intention."*

When one is confronted day after day with the things that must be done, it is easy to see how we fall away from our knowing, our intuitive nature energy. These energies are vital to us moving forward. Too many times we have been lost to the human condition, which is a very dense form of energy. That energy is familiar to us so that is why we keep falling back into the mundane, non-productive human condition issues that plague our life.

What "G" says is, *"Man goes to what is familiar because you don't have to think about it. You don't have to put any energy forward in it. It is what it is. That's why it's been difficult for man to change his ways, to take accountability for the very energy he denies."*

There are many ways to use our intuitive energy. I am clairvoyant, clairaudient, and clairsentient. I have learned how to connect and use the energy, which is something we all can do. I know that in my journey as a healer I constantly work with God energy. As an intuitive, one of the things I can do is see the etheric field around clients. I use their auras to help me determine what is for the highest good of the person that I am working with. I recognize that healing requires a lot of intuition and intuitive energy.

How did we, as individualized energy, ever come into existence? This was best explained by "G" in a channeling session.

"G" explained, *"Energy was void of substance at first and at one point in the vastness of all things, creation became aware of Its own existence and it was Good. This is what we call God/Source/Infinite Energy or God energy. Then this God energy reached out for more, not out of loneliness, but out of a desire to experience more in the vastness. So God made Light, Hue, and that also was good. This became the energy of Soul Spirit. This is also the speed of light. Hue is the feminine side, the female energy.*

Because the energy of the infinite could create, it then reached out and created Pitch, Sound. Pitch became the energy of Soul Mind, which is the masculine side, the male energy. It is also the speed of sound.

The energy of God and Good, the energy of Hue and Light and the energy of Pitch and Sound, all came together creating. It wasn't like an explosion, but more like the opening of a flower or the birth of a new plant breaking through the surface of the ground. And so Etheric Form became, which is the energy of Soul Body and is the unique soul energy (USE), an individualized essence. It is not a physical body yet. It is the etheric field or etheric energy that has now taken on USE.

What is the soul? It is the storehouse of information for the spirit, mind and body. It stores experience and cellular memory. Once the spirit is contained within the etheric body, it is unique, individualized. The soul mind is contained around the soul spirit giving it shape. Otherwise the soul spirit would dissipate all over the place. If anyone has seen digital pictures, you may have seen orbs of light captured somewhere in the photo. Cameras can take quicker shots than we can see. That's how it can capture the orbs. The orbs are the souls. It happens to appear as an orb in pictures because the soul is moving at the time the picture is taken. But souls can have many shapes. For anyone who can see spirit, it can be in the shape of physical bodies, etc.

Spirit just is. It has no real separation. It is what it is. It exists, yet it knows. It just doesn't have its unique flavor yet. Let's say you are working in an ice cream parlor and you begin to use all the same ingredients. At first it's just white content with all the ice and stuff. Then you begin to add the flavor - like chocolate, strawberry and vanilla. You then might add nuts, cookies or candy or other things to make it taste good. That is what it is like for spirit, for the USE to become unique.

In the very beginning of a USE's first incarnation, it doesn't have any experience. When it decides to densify and incarnate, it picks and chooses a physical body to reside in. Each USE chooses their physical characteristics such as eye color, hair color, weight, height, body shape and even gender. If more Hue pours into Form, the body is more female. If more Pitch pours into Form, the body is more male. Once it incarnates, it begins to get its experience, lifetime after lifetime and stores it in the USE. This information is brought with the USE into each incarnation."

USE is unique because there is not a single person just like you or me. We are the ones that travel this life, seeing it as only we can. This USE is the essence and personality of who we are here on earth in physical form as well as all the information experienced in this lifetime and every past lifetime that this USE has incarnated.

I have often asked myself the question, "Why do I get sick?" "Why do we choose to suffer?" Cancer, disease, lack, limitation is really a product of human condition, and that we, as USE, become caught in the cycle of creating without realizing that we're creating. It can also be a disruption of the natural flow of energy. If we have back pain for example, it can be because it's trying to tell us our body is out of sync or out of its natural rhythm. We are so affected by stress and day-to-day issues that sometimes we're not even aware that it's happening to us. So our body gives us signals and that what's that pain can be.

When we get too much energy or too much signal to an area, it can create a build up of energy at that site that can create health issues. Whatever the physical reason for the pain and suffering, it is a signal to let us know that there's something in our life that needs to be looked at or taken care of.

Recall that human condition is being unaware of our God power within. It is really all of the day-to-day human experience that we give priority to when we use our own creative power and energy, rather than using God energy. We don't even know we're doing it. We're in the dark. They're old patterns of behavior that have become so much a part of us that we do them without thought. It's a reaction instead of a conscious choice. When we start asking the question, "Why did I do this?" we are becoming aware of patterns in our life because we're finally awakening from being asleep.

We forget our birthright. We forget where we came from. And we begin to get into a place where we say things like, "It must be God's will that I have cancer" or "It must be God's will that my sister had a stroke." But in the true essence of the journey, these conditions are created by the lack of awareness, the lack of clarity, and the lack of taking accountability for how we use the energy that is given to us.

It basically tells us that we choose things based on what we've been taught, based on things we believe, based on the type of information we take in and learn from. For example, parents, family, friends, coworkers, school, television, religion, media, books, etc., anything we have ever come into contact with, goes into us and we hold to it as fact. This is all energy we exude. Human condition is basically stored in emotional energy. That's why most physical conditions stem from emotional issues.

We are very good at storing history, but not very accurate. We are good at holding on to what we perceive as the story. Remember earlier I mentioned that everyone's story is different because of their experience, their level of awareness and their understanding. Basically, the more we fall away from our power of energy, the more we separate from our unique God energy, the further we are from perfection, perfect health, abundance, happiness, and joy.

Originally, when USE was created, it was given free will, spirit's will. And in that moment of its creation, immediately upon its birth as a man or woman, it began to lose something. It separated itself from God. The more that we incarnated, the more we repeated patterns diminishing our ability to communicate with God and the more we began to fall into the rhythm of lack. We could no longer see ourselves as a part of God energy. This resulted in the creation of low self worth and non-deservance within humankind. And so began the journey of feeling like we are failures.

What are failures? The misuse of energy. What is a mistake? It is a misdirection of energy. The true awareness of all this is really about recognizing that life is correctable. And how do we correct it? We correct it by recognizing that we misused the energy and we do what we can to right it. We can't always right it immediately. For example, if we murdered someone, we can't bring that person back to life. However, we can learn from the mistake and work at changing who we are so that we don't repeat that same behavior or lesson. And obviously, with the laws on this planet, we would have to pay the consequences for that act.

God doesn't have to punish us for consequences made here. Man, even with the misuse of energy, has created consequences. Is it right or wrong? No. Why, we ask? Because God sees everything as a learning experience. If we stand by goodness, that is the use of God energy.

When we remain in the real light of God energy, we would never harm or wrong another person because we would be connected to God energy and that desire would never fill our heart or our being. Rather, we would honor, respect and care for that other being.

If we harm someone, it is misusing the very energy from which we are created. The desire to harm another is because a young soul has chosen a road of lessons. These lessons will play out in this lifetime and into the next if it is not corrected or righted this time around. If we kill someone, we must pay for it because this is how the world works. It believes in an eye for an eye and a tooth for a tooth. What I understand it to be is that we need to educate, to teach, to rise up out of the human condition and this nonproductive use of energy and create a world in which the whole of this existence is based out of the correct use of God love energy.

In spirit, there is no right or wrong. God sees it as just a series of learning possibilities. But to harm another is removing our self so far from the God energy that we feel lost. Many lose their sense of recognizing what is right or wrong in man's eyes when this happens.

Energy itself does not define right or wrong. In the eyes of creation, it is all used as a way of expanding and growing, contracting and changing. Do we love all energy? People do not, but God does. Do we love all people, all humankind? People do not, but God does. Is there judgment? By people, yes, but by God, no. God only loves.

God has been defined as wrathful when people are bad and joyous when they are good. But that in itself becomes a manipulation doesn't it? If we hold for the highest good for all, does that not bring the highest good for all? Yes.

You see, it really comes down to defining the energy of unconditional love. "G" tells us, *"If all the human beings, masters, angels, spirits in the heavens were to come together in unconditional love, the whole of unconditional love could not fit into the all of God. It would be bigger. There would be no room for hurting and suffering. Man would finally understand the true gift of life.*

When people are walking and utilizing the infinite energy, using the mind energy in such a way that the spirit energy can reach its fullest potential, the physical form/body comes to a place of creating the kind of life that we desire. We must hold hope, divine hope and keep holding love for all. Don't we all know that love perpetuates more love? If all humans held the true essence of unconditional love, then it would instill more love and goodness in the world. The energy of God, when held at its highest, illuminates, becomes a beacon, becomes the very essence of what man craves. So I say, let's not crave. Let's create. God holds divine hope.

Energy, plain and simple, never sits idle. It is a constant, just like God. That is why I say, stand and hold to the highest standards of this life, for our USE is our part in creating in the universe. So create wisely. Create with the knowing in our heart that as long as we are moving towards unconditional love, we will have achieved our birthright. This is where energy needs to be focused, needs to have a set intention to the road. It desires to be useful, just like man. It desires to have purpose, just like man. It desires to know the what and the why of its existence. God defines the when and the how of it.

Channeling by "G"
"Energy"

Note: The following text is transcribed from an actual channeling by "G". The content and grammar is written as spoken by "G".

"G": Hello, this is "G". Tonight's segment is on energy. In our last segment, we talked about birthright. This part is about our use of this energy and how you transform the journey by understanding the original point of energy and how it is used.

"G": Hello, everyone.
All: Hello, "G".
"G": Welcome.

"G": Energy is the foundation of all things for there is energy in every part of creation. You see, energy is creation. What you do with it is how you control that energy. Think about your day to day life. You get up, you get out of bed, you look at the day, you go forward, and when you walk out into the world, all around you there is energy. There is energy from light. There is energy from sound. There is energy even in the simplest things like a chair or a car. Think about all the things around you. Everything that you experience has a form of energy. You think about God, Source. You think about the Infinite. It in itself is the foundation of creation and is the foundation of energy. Even in the vast void in the beginning something changed, and it became aware.

Q: "G," would you please explain what Source or Infinite energy means?

"G": Absolutely. Source or Infinite energy is God. It is what you call all good. In the very beginning, what they call the big bang, (it really was not a big bang; it really was very quiet) it was like all mass of denseness and all that started to shift and change, move together. It was through that that all of a sudden God became aware of Itself. It woke up into Its knowing. And it was in that moment that It woke up, that It was Good.

Q: "G," is there energy that is good and bad?

"G": Well think of it as the misuse of energy or the lack of use of energy. See, all things are created. It is really how you use the energy of Good. As I explained in the first segment of this book or this series of talks about birthright and co-creation and the energy of co-creation, there is this part where everything has intention, everything has a point of origin, and that starts with you.

You think about God, this unconditionally loving God who loves you for who you are and that is all that it knows, this God that gives you everything that you ask. Think about being a co-creator. Think about being a person who has come into this life and the whole series of creations that you have made. It's like that. So, when you are using energy, the same energy that gave you life, you see, that very same energy that gives you all that you ask is also the energy that will take it away because you are the one who decides what to do with it.

There is a statement that Ernest Holmes wrote that says, "That which makes you sick, also heals you." See, it is not defined by one greater or less. It's not like you have a bunch of rules out there that float around you, only one.

And that is the original point of energy, creation. The use of creation is, "I will go forward and create my life by the words I speak, by thoughts, by feelings, and emotions. And it is through that creative energy that all of a sudden I have created my life.

Think about a man who wakes up one day, gets out of bed, and the first thing he greets is feeling good about his day. Then he goes out and his car won't start. Now, he has a choice, does he not? Does he not have a choice of how he is going to accept the fact that his car does not start?

So, think about that. You go forward in life and something happens that you feel is out of your control. Well, it really isn't. It is all a series of events that bring it to a point of recognition and where you recognize the choices you have made in life. If your car breaks down, you have a choice. Do you get mad or do you recognize in that moment there is something you have done to create the outcome? Maybe it was a fear that you were going to wake up and your battery was going to be dead. Maybe you even thought it because the battery light looked a little low and you thought, "Well, you know, my battery must not be working very good," and you don't think anything more about it. But at the moment when you thought it, the energy of creation said, "So be it." You get up and go out, and guess what? Your car battery is dead. That is the use or misuse of energy.

Q: So, "G", I understand how I've created something. How can I seem to fix it?

"G": How you change something that you have already put into motion is by first recognizing that you have already set into motion something that has had an outcome. Correct? The second thing you do to rectify something that would be a negative would be to stop and say "33 second rule". By saying "33 second rule" within 33 seconds of saying any words you have spoken that are negative, you are telling the Universe that you did not mean it and the Universe honors that. You see, God has a soft spot for all of you and this is something he created because of that soft spot.

You know, like I was telling the last group of people that were with "G", when you think about God and you truly think about your life and all the things that have happened to you, have you really truly hit bottom? Have you really truly experienced the very bottom of your life? No. Somehow, some way, you have always had something lift you up, something happened that maybe made the fall not so painful. You think about your life. Yes, you are a co-creator, but thank God that God has a soft spot. I know some people don't believe that it is so because they feel their life is so bad. The reason they don't believe it is because they stay in that perpetual state of lack.

Q: Would these be people that consider themselves to have bad luck?

"G": Absolutely. You think about that statement. What does the Universe hear when you say, "You know, if I didn't have bad luck, I wouldn't have any luck at all." Do you hear that statement? Do you hear people say that?

Well, think about the world and think about the Universe. Like I said in birthright, God does not see counterfeit money. It just sees money. That's why I say to you, when you are creating in your life, when you are using the energy of Source, of Infinite energy, this will bring you the desire that you put forth. Regardless of whether you believe in lack or you believe in abundance, the Universe does not define what you have. It has a rule. That rule says that whatever you ask for is granted. If you are creating lack, that is a misuse of the creative energy because you are creating a negative in your life. God says, "Well, I have to grant it to them because I love them unconditionally." It is man's misuse of himself because man is the one that chooses good or bad, not God. You pick abundance or you pick lack. You see?

Q: We have been talking about energy. Is there a difference in how fast something is created or the level of creation, depending upon the emotion that is behind it?

"G": Absolutely. Think about energy as a whole. It is constant yet it can be used in greater or lesser amounts. You know how when you turn on your hair dryer? You go Low, Medium, or High? The levels of different energy are like that. Yes? But it is still the same energy. It is but you bringing it into each level. You see it just continues to grow or it diminishes and goes down.

Q: "G", in that case, would you help me to understand why everyone's energy is different?

"G": Absolutely. Like I was saying, if you have many levels of dials on a particular device like your stove and you have all the way from '0' all the way up to 'broil', it is all in how you dial the energy. Mankind is the same way. Some people, you know you see them and they are like hyperactive, like somebody put them on overdrive and they just go, go, go. Yes? And then there are some people who are like "turtles", and you wonder if someone could just put a little fire under that one because that one is a really slow one. But you see it is all in the momentum of each person. They choose the energy by which they come and go. You know, it's like you might know someone who seems a little bit on the fast side and it never fails. You meet them and it's like talk, talk, talk, and they are gone. You're still in the conversation but they are long gone because they were finished. Have you ever done that?

Q: How is it then, "G", that you say people are different, but those very same people can be different even in the same day with the amount of energy that they are using?

"G": How it works is like this. Think about the different levels of how energy stands. Energy itself is like you have the different volts in a battery. You have different volts of energy that comes into a house, you know 110 or 220, and it just keeps going at the different levels.

Well, you see energy from outside stays as a constant energy. It comes in and hits a circuit and that circuit only allows a certain amount of power to get in because you don't want to blow your house up if it can only take in so many watts. Have you ever seen a light bulb go "bloop", like that? It's because it reached its point. Yes?

Well, people, you all have that. When babies are born, they are so full of energy and they are learning and growing and keep going but as you get older, it seems like the energy slows, you don't move as fast. It's like everything has its momentum. And because you believe this, because you have come here with the understanding that everything is born and everything dies, is that not the momentum you set in place?

So you see, that is part of the misunderstanding. If you are truly the all-powered energy there is, you could live forever, at least in the knowing that I know of Source energy. But you have not yet come to that place of truly believing that you are that energy.

Q: Can we talk about regeneration then, to live that long, and how we can do that?

"G": Well, I can touch on it and give you as much as I can. It's still up to how much you are able to understand. What you need to understand is that your words, your thoughts, your feelings, your emotions, every part of who you are, everything you have learned, everything that you have been taught, every avenue of learning is now inside of you. You have been taught, "It runs in the family." "It's genetic, you know, you have a grandmother that lived to be 102 while you have another parent that died at 57." What happens?

These things are what you have come to understand. If they say, "You know, the people in our family live a long life," and if you are told that, I guarantee you, you will be one of those people that get really old. But the moment that you hear, "you know, most people barely make it to 60," what happens? It sets in motion an understanding and you take it in as fact. Then you begin to create those things with that energy, the very words, the understanding that you have learned.

That is why I say the energy of Source light, this energy, is how you use it. If you believe that you have no power, then you have no power, but if you believe you are powerful, you are powerful. That is why I tell you most human beings only understand at the level of their awareness.

Q: So, I was taught energy can be created and destroyed. Is that true or what happens?

"G": You can never destroy energy. Energy is constant. But you can, like this physical body, destroy what is inside of it. But the energy of you, your unique soul energy, will always be. It just continues on to the next life. So, think about that. You know people are born and people die, and they choose a disease or they choose an illness. You have to understand, at the level of spirit, there is no disease, there is no illness, there is no suffering. This is created down here on earth because the longer you are here, the further away from God you have become.

Q: You just mentioned unique soul energy. Can you clarify that a little bit more?

"G": Absolutely. You see, unique soul energy is the unique personality, the unique you. It was in the beginning, when God became aware, so to speak, that Source all of a sudden realized It existed. It began to create a series to things, not out of loneliness, but out of a sense of learning. And so God, unique soul energy was created from the different energies out there. We have Hue, which is Light; that is feminine. Then He created Sound, or Pitch, which is masculine. God and Pitch and Hue came together and created form, body, man. This is where unique soul energy resides, in you. It is where the information of all your life experience and all the lifetimes you have lived, are held and recorded. So, whenever you shed the body of the physical and go back into Source, when you come back again and create another body, the information is still held in this unique soul energy.

Q: Are the DNA and the atoms related to the body and energy?

"G": Unique soul energy is like a book of information, a book of facts. The fact is, you have made choices in this life that you have lived. You know how you write in journals or you write in your books to keep your history going or you have your big computers with all your data bases in it? This unique soul energy is a giant data base for all the many lifetimes you have lived, the many times that you have incarnated, both past life and parallel. So, you see, all the things you have ever experienced in your life, this lifetime and many past lifetimes, are all recorded in this space.

Q: "G", I can barely remember what I did last week so how can I remember what happened in another lifetime? I certainly don't remember it right now.

"G": Well, think of it like this. How many of you have had a personal experience in life where you go along and all of a sudden you are walking and something seems familiar and you don't know why? It's like you look at a house and say "I know that house. How do I know that house?"

Think about those things. That moment was a moment when you became aware of a past life experience or maybe you have a conversation and immediately you say "Oh, I think I'm having deja vu because this is so familiar. I have done this before. I have had this conversation." Yes, you have, because this unique soul energy, this body, this you, has all the memory of all those things. That is part of why, when you think about something that happens to you and you don't understand why, it is because it is not anything that you thought you created in this lifetime. Sometimes karma is that one thing that you create as a way of 'paying back' people that you may have wronged in this lifetime or the next or maybe in the past. You see? Karma is basically man's way of justifying a wrong.

Q: Is our unique soul energy the same in every lifetime or does it change?

"G": You, as the person, changes, but the information is still the same. That is why I say I know that there are thousands and thousands of years of knowledge locked away inside this very unique soul spirit and this unique soul spirit knows what it knows. You don't have to take the road of suffering, the road of lack, the hard road because you have already done it.

Q: "G", how can I get that knowledge out of me?

"G": Well, think about when you are a student in school. You are going along and you've got your books and you've got your stuff and it's interesting how you have this information inside of you, correct? And as you get older, you go along and you get so far away from it and say, "Oh, my God, that was so long ago". Well, that information is still in you, but what brings it back to you is something that reminds you. Think about math. Now everyone has done math. Yes? You've taken classes, you've done the math piece. Is it not interesting that if you sit down and watch the math problem play out a few times, it comes back to you and you go, "Oh, I remember this". That is how it is.

You see, it's still there. You just have to keep doing a series of things in your life to re-awaken it. It's already there, like the math you did when you were young. Part of the reason why people lose it is because they stop using it. So, now it is time to keep using it, keep remembering it, keep moving forward. That is why man has this thing that says, "I need to know, I need to know". It's like an energy that keeps saying "I've got to go forward, I need to know." This is what makes you find it, like an explorer, yes?

Q: So is this need to know more like remembering an event that happened, like I remember something? Is that similar to the gut feeling or the intuition?

"G": Yes. It's like this. How many times have you gone through your life and all of a sudden somebody says, "Let's do this," and your gut says, "Don't do it." And you don't listen to it. Then you go out and do it and you go, "I should have listened. I knew this was going to happen."

This is the same thing. It is memories. Psychic ability is a form of energy. Everyone has a birthright to it because it is your right to know, it is your right to be connected to God and Source. It is your right as a human being becoming that you are granted this gift. But it is through a series of lifetimes, a series of events, that you either squash it or some people make it happen.

You know how some, you go to them and they say, "I have a message," or you go to different people who have psychic ability or that are intuitive or have intuition and they know things? It's like different levels of knowing. Well, these things for some are very easy because they were never suppressed. They were never held down or told, "Bad, wrong, no!" The moment you hear, "bad, wrong, no," you push it away because of the old pattern of judgment which is wrong, yet so imbedded in you.

But yet, you know what? You still have it because you have a knowing. Have you ever had a moment where you thought about somebody and all of a sudden the phone rang and it was them? Have you ever had a feeling about something and all of a sudden it happens? This is basic right to spirit.

Q: Is that why it seems like some psychics are more accurate than others and their timelines never seem to be on target? Could you put some clarity around that, please?

"G": Absolutely. You see, psychic ability is developed, practiced. You know, "G" says practice, practice makes perfect. Well, it does. Think about a surgeon. Would you want a surgeon who has not practiced what he was going to do? I think you would be a little nervous going under that. You see, practice makes you better at what you do. It makes you the best. So, I say practice. But sometimes, in practicing, you know you have a psychic that gives accurate information and they go forward. It's like, "Wow, how do they get this?" It's because they have developed the connection to Source, Light, God.

Now, you have to understand timelines, because time does not exist in Source or Light, or Spirit. That is a man made thing. See, you come down, you have a sunrise and sunset, you live and die. You see these things that keep cycling back and forth that tells you, like seasons - you go through spring, summer, fall, and winter. So you sit there in your head going, "Well, that's another year gone by." And so begins this timeline thing.

But you see, where spirit is, time does not exist. And the interesting thing about it is that because time does not exist, and because you have free will, the person who is giving you the information could be close, but maybe not right on. Or maybe they're off by a long shot. That is because you have a choice to go a different way down the road or a choice to change your circumstances.

There are a billion outcomes to one event which is why it's so difficult to truly predict the 'end of the world' as people say. How do you truly predict that? How do you know what's going to happen when in one course of your life you could go this way and completely change the outcome. So life is really a series of events that you choose and pick along the road.

Q: "G", we talk about energy, a personal energy. How does that differ from electrical energy or other energies that are out there?

"G": Well, you see, energy is energy. It all comes from one thing. What is different about you, the unique soul energy, is that you are identified and aware and you know who you are whereas electricity is not defined. It is not knowing.

See, spirit alone, just the word spirit, just is. It's not unique. It's not special. It just is. So you see, that is what happens. All energy out there is not defined yet but you have defined you. You all of a sudden became and said "Oh! This is me and now I go forward and learn." Electricity, or even a beam of light or sound, which is also energy, all have something in common, but they do not have uniqueness.

Q: Why is it that some people feel energy more than others, or that they will say, "Did you feel the energy in the room?" Yet others don't feel it at all.

"G": Think about the senses, the six senses. Think about touch. To some people, touch is very important; the hands feel everything. They are very sensitive, whereas another person hardly feels anything at all. It seems like that kind of person can prick their finger and it doesn't bother them. Another person pricks their finger and they think it's the end of the world. All these things are because each part of this touch is unique, correct? Each person has different levels of it.

Just like you think about smell. Somebody says "I tell you, my beak don't smell nothing. It's like plugged up or something. (sniff, sniff) Nothing came out." And another person can walk in the room and tell you what perfume that person had on, whether or not the person had a cigarette. They can tell you what the person ate for dinner that night because their sense, their nose, is like a supersonic smeller. You see? So, you think about that.

Each one of them, like the person who comes into a room who says "God, do you feel the energy in this room?" and someone else says "What the heck are you talking about?" and they look at you like you grew a horn, two of them actually. You see, those things are because each person has their own way of understanding energy.

Some people are what they call clairvoyant. Clairvoyant is just, they see....they see light, they see auras, they see your body, they see the etheric field, they see all the colors around you. Another person would look at you and say, "What the heck are you talking about?" Then you have someone who says "Did you hear that?" And you go, "I didn't hear a thing." It's because they are clairaudient. They can hear spirit, vibration, or sound.

Then there are others who have developed clairsentient, which is a knowing inside themselves. They don't know where the information came from. All of a sudden it just is and they know what they know. They speak the words and people go "Are you in my head? How do you know that about me?" You see?

Each person has their own way of developing that energy or not. It is all relative to how this person has gone forward. If they have a fear, that can also stop a person from being intuitive or being psychic. Maybe your family of origin said, "The devil made me do it. That's bad." Other people come into it and they say, "Oh, yeah, it runs in the family. Grandma, grandpa, everybody has the ability." So, of course it's going to be in you. You see, it is all in what you've learned, what you understand it to be.

You define you. You define your energy by other people, by your life, by the things you read. All of that defines how big your energy is or how small your energy is. The more you place the filters of human condition on you, the smaller the energy of you is. You need to shed the energy of human condition so that you can rise up to be the birthright of your life.

Q: What is human condition? Can you talk about that a little bit more?

"G": Human condition is all the things that you have lived in this lifetime and all the others. Human condition is like, "It's genetic". Your mother says, "Well, you know, it runs in our family. You come from fat stock." That's a human condition.

Think about somebody having cancer or depression. "You know, I will tell you, your Uncle Fred and your Aunt Marge and all these people around have this depression. It runs in the family. You know, it's just a matter of time before you get it."

Another condition, you watch your television, and all of a sudden it tells you you've got "indigestion." The first thing you do is run out and buy that nice pink bottle of stuff or those round little pills that you take because maybe some day you're going to have that. The Universe hears that and so it goes forward and you go out and create this.

Think about religion, another filter. Think about what you have been taught in your life about religion. "God is judging and you'd better be good because He is up there keeping track." Another filter. "Thou shalt not bear false witness against your neighbor. You shouldn't lie. The moment you lie, you're doomed. You might as well just check out, that's it." But see, these are all filters.

Think about what friends have said. "You know, I've got to tell you. This PMS stuff is really getting to me. I really have a problem with PMS." And you think, what the heck is PMS? And they say, "You know, that's when you're bloating right around that time of the month and you have all this stuff going on. You know, I get so cranky. I bite people's heads off, too." And you sit there and go, "You know, I do that too." And all of a sudden you have PMS and you didn't even know what that was. You thought it was a TV channel like CNN. But because you listened to your friend who says she's got this, you get it. So you see, that's a human filter, human condition.

Each one of these filters builds on top of the other and your energy, your unique soul energy, your divine spirit energy comes through all of that. When it comes through all those filters, what do you think happens to it? It finally gets to where it's supposed to be, but by the time it gets there it's just a little itty bitty tiny light because it just can't take it anymore.

It might have started out like a big, beaming light, like you see the big old lighthouses on the coast of the ocean so ships won't crash in. Well, all of a sudden that great big beam of light is like a little, little dot, like a little flashlight. You know the little keychain lights that are like a little dot? That's what you've got by the time the spirit filters through all the baggage, all the crap, all the things that you have put in its way. So it is stuck in this body with limited resources because of all those things that you allow to squash the spirit.

Q: What about when you are in a room with a number of people judging and maybe gossiping? How do you keep the spirit alive in that kind of an environment?

"G": Very good question. The number one thing you must remember is that each time you come into a room, you have a choice. You have a choice of whether or not you are going to let that person say things or do things to affect you. You have a choice of whether or not you feed that information. Correct? Have you ever gotten into gossip? Think about that. Then all of a sudden you have someone talking bad about someone else and you feed the bad and the next thing you know you got this whole kind of thing going.

The difference is, someone who has finally awakened the spirit within realizes that they are not going there. They will not feed this energy because they know that the moment they feed this energy, they are sucked into human condition. You don't want to be there because you know that human condition is the #1 thing, like a big old thumb on the top of your head that's pushing you right into the ground. And there you sit, trying to break the surface to see the light, but human condition is just holding you right there. That's how it is.

Q: So what you're saying is - human condition affects body, mind, and spirit? Can you talk a little bit more about all three?

"G": Yes. Think about your spirit, yes? It is out there in its beautiful light and you're unique. You're just kind of being you and really liking it and you're bored. Here you are, you're this loving little baby and you're all happy. Of course you cry because you're scared with people coming around and you hear all this noise and you don't know what it is at first. But this loving little voice says, "Oh, my beautiful baby, I love you," and you just feel all happy. You see? That's good.

But you see, something happens because that unique spirit, it's laying there and being all loved up and held and it's all cute, you know. That unique soul energy all of a sudden experiences something negative. It experiences its first bath. It has never had one before and so it screams. It gets scared, you know? So maybe that soul/spirit says "What is this? I don't know what this is." Fear, fear, fear, fear, fear.

But even in that moment I will tell you what that is. Unique soul energy has a memory. Do you know what that memory is? That memory might be past life, maybe that child or that person drowned in a past life and because, like I said earlier, this unique soul energy stores all experience that this soul has been through, the child has a fear of water and so it cries. And so it begins the cycle of fear. It never experienced it before in this lifetime, but yet it is stored somewhere in the soul mind.

What is the mind? What is the mind energy? The mind energy is your mind's choice. What does that mean? Mind's choice is where you decide - right, left, good, bad, up, down. Do you see? Your mind is the one that helps you to decide whether you are going to be fearful or not. You see, the mind feels the emotion of fear and says, "Oh, yeah, this is fear. This is scary." And the mind says, "We need to remember that one because when we go back there, we'll have to draw on that memory." Right?

So what happens? Down the road this baby starts to grow up and it starts to crawl and it's pretty happy. It kind of got over the whole fear of water because mom and dad and everybody kept washing and nothing happened. So the baby got over it because it had a positive experience with water. It learned to play and stuff like that.

But, what happens when the baby all of a sudden realizes, "You know, this crawling just isn't cutting it, so now I've got to try and pull myself up. I'm going to use my muscles." And all of a sudden that baby pulls himself up into a standing position. You know how babies wobble and wiggle, trying to just stay up, and they fall down and it hurts, and they cry. And all of a sudden the mind goes, "Oh, that hurt, better remember that." So the baby crawls a little bit longer because falling was just too painful. But some babies go, "Ok, that might have hurt a little bit, but not enough to keep me down." And the next time they get up they are a little stronger and a little steadier. They have a little more stability under their feet and the next thing you know they start to walk.

Now remember, the mind is storing this information. Everything that happens to this unique soul energy baby is being stored as information. It remembers everything that happens to it, everything. And you say, "I don't even remember what happened yesterday. How the heck does that happen?" I will tell you what it is. Mankind puts in this safety valve that says, "Don't remember that hurt, but don't forget that it might happen again." I like that one. Ok, that's a trick. So you see, you kind of cornered yourself ... forget/don't forget, forget/don't forget. You get a little confused.

See, what happens is the spirit, what we call short term memory, forgets it. That long term memory...it's stored way back there and if something happens, it goes "boom" right back to you and you go, "I remember this. How do I remember this? What is this? I feel this." So you see, it's like long term/short term.

I know it's not quite how the real mind works, but it's the best way I can describe the spirit and how it stores and carries things, you see? In short term memory, you wouldn't remember a thing, but long term memory.... You know how it gets there? Repeat patterns. That's how the mind remembers, repeat patterns.

You know how the baby kept getting up and falling down and getting up and falling down? Well, that long term memory says, "Oh, that getting up and falling down, yeah, I remember that." But the short term memory forgets how painful it was. So, all of a sudden you're walking and you're going through life. You've got your legs working and now you're not a baby anymore. Now you're five years old. And this spirit says, "Oh, I'm five. I know so much." But you see, it does, because the baby remembers just like the five year old remembers. It remembers where it came from. It remembers all these things. It is here to learn. It is here to experience life.

Q We're always told that we have to let the past go because it's past and we can't do anything about it. So, how can we let the past go if it's all stored in the mind and it keeps coming back?

"G": This is where "G" comes in. You see, the mind is really not your enemy. What it is, is that the mind really is misused. The mind is really choices. Correct? Think about what your mind does. You mind processes information. It goes through all these things. It takes things in.

Think about the journey of life, yes? How many times have you walked in life and you've had regret. You say, "Why do I keep doing this to myself? You know, I should have known that person was not good for me. But there I go. I find the same kind of person every time. You know, I must have a sign on me that says, 'I take losers'." You hear your words, right? And you ask the question, "How do I forget?"

It's part of healing. You have to find your way back through it all to the original point of your beginning - your spirit's will. You know how they say that God gave you free will? God did give you free will. God gave you the ability to choose your life and go forward. Yes? Then man gets into human condition. Remember the TV and people and religion and all that stuff? That is where all of mind's choice resides.

You know that committee in your head that talks to you? When you go to do something and your mind goes, "You know, I really wouldn't do that if I were you. You're not too bright. What if you screw it up?" And so you think, "Maybe I shouldn't do it. What if I screw it up?" What if you do? What does that mean? Think about your life. Have you made mistakes? Have you fallen down? Have you picked yourself up? So, is that not something that you can correct?

Think about a mistake. A mistake is something you can correct. The use of energy means that co-creation says, "I am a co-creator with God and use of that energy means that I am out creating whatever my life desires." But see, you can't create from the mind, not really.

What you have to begin to do is create from your spirit. You ask how? I'll tell you how. The mind, as you know, has information. Correct? It knows things. You can't let the mind govern you. Your spirit is the one that has to govern you. Your spirit uses the data base of information to correct the direction, to move forward in life, to make right choices in your journey instead of letting your mind run rampant, like a crazy person, screaming through your head going, "No, don't do it. Fear, fear, fear." And you go "Fear, fear, fear. I'm not going to do it. I'm scared." And the spirit says, "Why are you afraid?" "Well, because, bad, bad." And the spirit says "OK, bad."

So what you have to start to do is recognize that the mind is but a tool. It is not the one to do the choosing. The spirit is. Let the spirit guide the information. Instead of letting your mind guide you, let your sprit guide you. Your spirit knows what is in your highest good. Your spirit knows what is best for you because it is not in its filters. It is not lost in repeat patterns of runaway feelings or runaway thoughts. It knows that it is a co-creator. It knows what it must do in order to make a dynamic life grand.

But what you do is you fall back into old patterns of your life. You let the mind become the governor instead of the spirit. Think about that. How many people have had someone in power that was not so good? Have you ever put someone in power and then went, "Oh, my God. Why did we do this?" Well, think about your mind. You put it in power and then you sit there and go, "Well, that was stupid." It's still your mind.

Your heart says, "You have become aware that you placed the wrong one in power and now it is time to say 'no'. My spirit's will is my divine spirit. My divine spirit is my co-creation, my connection to God. It is my image and likeness of. So, if I am to stand in the energy of Source or Infinite energy, then I must shed human condition. I must cast out all the bad habits that I have gotten myself into so that I don't continue to repeat patterns over and over and over again.

It's about recognition and recognizing you. You need to claim your birthright. You need to command the energy of the Infinite. You need to take hold of these things and not let life suppress you, hold you down. You know, I know we have talked about a lot of things just now and one of the greatest things you have to remember is that you, your self, have choice. But what you have to remember in that choice is - do you choose from the mind or do you allow your spirit's will to be the guiding factor in the journey?

Someone asked the question of "G" a while ago, ""G", if God or Source, Infinite energy is all loving and you say there is no right or wrong, but only a series of learning events, how do you get past someone who commits murder?" Well, you have to understand that murder in its whole, God does not judge that. But man has put in place a series of things that makes people have to be accountable for the event.

Think about your unique soul energy holding all that information, past life and present. Let's say you go out into the world and because you're a young soul and in the learning mode of your life, you do a heinous thing like killing someone. Well, of course, you have laws here that say you must pay penance for what you have done.

But you see, you've also done that in your own spirit. Man has created what's called karma. And karma is your judgment. You put yourself into this. You say, "I have committed a wrong so I must right it." Then you die. They put you to death, you know, because man says 'an eye for an eye, a tooth for a tooth'. All of a sudden you come back in the next lifetime and you meet this person and the person kills you because the wrong has to be righted. Not always is it exactly the same. Maybe it's just suffering, not only in this lifetime or the next, but maybe it's paid by this one or that one.

So you see? How can you sit in judgment of someone who is sick? Think about a person who has mental illness, someone who has no idea because they are so young in the journey. See, prisons, to me, while I don't think they are wrong, what I believe they have done is begun to create the exact thing that they are trying to stop. They create a series of criminals because they put them back into it instead of teaching them the ability to co-create, the ability of their spirit, teaching them about light, teaching them about the journey.

Some people go into prison and are transformed because they are still so close to the light. But there are some that have been so far removed from the light and it has filtered through so much that the light is like the little itty bitty light of a flashlight on a keychain. If that light is so small, sometimes it's hard to see. Why not educate? I have always said if you feed a man for a day, he eats for a day. But if you teach a man to fish, he learns to feed himself for a lifetime.

People need to learn about this. People need to understand that this journey in life is a continuation of a series of events that, each time it happens, there is a choice made. Which way do I go? Do I follow the light or do I continually fall back into that human condition, that mundane thought, that repeat pattern? I have talked about it in birthright, how everything you do is an outcome.

Q: "G", earlier on you had mentioned that energy is constant. Does that mean that it doesn't move, it just sits stagnant or how does that work?

"G": Energy as a whole never sits idle. It is constantly moving one way or another, expanding, contracting, in motion all the time. Think about when you look out into the night sky and you look up and see a star that's trillions of miles away. That light energy has found its way to your eye. That is how powerful the energy of light is.

And think about sound. When you listen to it, that sound travels and hits the ear, then reverberates back. So sunlight and music are all constant, yet they are only two examples. The energy is constantly bouncing off, moving and going. It is continually transforming.

The same light that was sent to your eye was sent back out into the universe and found someone else. So, think about that when you are looking at the stars at night. Think about the sound of music and how it feels inside of you. Think about how much the energy of all things is continually moving and expanding in so many ways.

Q: "G", can you explain light and sound?

"G": Yes. I talk about light as being that sense of feminine, yes? Light itself was created, we call it 'Hue', and that Hue or light is the spirit. The spirit just kind of is. It does not really have any distinction at all, but the very light that goes out is the very light of all existence. Then you have what we call 'Pitch' or sound, and that, too, is unique in its own energy. It is the essence of the masculine. Light is faster. It can move very fast. It's very quick. Sound is a little slower, a little less fast, yet they both have an impact.

Think about how sound can shatter glass if it hits a certain note. Light can burn if it is at a certain magnification.

So you see, they both have the power to destroy and they also have the power to give life. It's all in how you use them. If you use light for good, if you use light not to magnify and burn, but to emulate and give light to the journey, think of how beautiful the road can be. And think about sound, how the music reverberates and the energy of that sound moving out bathes you in this sense.

You know how you listen to music and all of a sudden you get goosebumps on your arm when it hits a certain note? That is your sound. If you feel your body responding as the music plays, it is your song, your mantra, your vibration. That is how you know when you are in that place. But even sound, as it has its place, it fills the place of light.

Q: In our world there is so much sound, in our cities, in our homes, with so many people. How does one have balance with all the energies that are coming at us?

"G": Think about a choice. Do you not choose to put on your TV set or your music? Do you not choose to turn your lights on or off? Just like all things, you cannot stop them. They are out there in existence, but you do have a choice of whether or not you allow that impact to affect who you are as a person. I always say that you are but an actor upon the stage and if you don't like what is being played, change the script, get off the stage, make a choice.

Don't stand there in the vibration of all these things feeling helpless or lost. Rise up out of this human condition, rise up out of the mayhem of sound and light and draw to you, create with this, the perfect balance of light and sound.

Don't turn your TV set on if it is too noisy in the day. Sit in quiet contemplation but remember, even in the greatest silence there is still sound. So listen to what is in the silence. Look and see what is out there.

I always say look at the sunrise, look at the sunset. Experience the light in so many different ways because when the sun rises, you see Hue in all its glory. Listen to the birds sing, hear the Pitch and the music around you because in the morning, do you not hear the birds sing at the rise of light? Together, do they not create the most amazing thing? So, that's how you must see that light has its place, sound has its place, and together they are magnificent. No one dawn or sunset is ever exactly the same. When you reach out and experience the whole of it, it is different every day.

Think about your life. Is not every day different? Is not every day magnificent? So, let's go forward in that. Let's heal that. Let's know that as a unique soul energy, you are gathering data for God. You are gathering information for Infinite so you become the record of all things. Don't cry and give up and be sad because you made wrong choices in life. Have not those choices brought you where you are today? Have they not wakened you to a new life? Have they not given you something in return? So, don't see it as a negative. See the gift in it. See the joy in it. See the positive in it because there always is one.

Q: "G", if I were to clear out my filters, how would it affect my energy?

"G": When you start to clear filters, the human condition, each time you remove a filter - think about your family of origin. You know the 'it runs in the family' comment? Let's say you clear that out and you no longer accept that possibility. Your health improves which improves your energy.

Think about if somebody says to you, "You're not very smart," but you refuse to accept that and you go beyond it and say, "I am brilliant." Well, that again changes the energy and all of a sudden you are brilliant. See, you are all these things because you believe them to be so. If you remove those things that hold you down, suppress you, what happens?

Think about a top. You know, those things that you push up and down and they go really, really fast? If you hold onto the sides it doesn't go, does it? But if you push down on it, does it not start to spin? And the more you push on it, the faster it goes. Well, think of the hands or things that touch it that cause it to slow or to stop. Those are filters. Remove the conditions which you have placed there.

Remember the lady that did not know what PMS was but accepted it when it was explained to her? That affects her and so she has health issues. Think about money, the energy of money. It is very, very important in this society and in this world. You know it's like the world revolves around money. That's kind of what has been said, yes?

Think about a child that comes from poverty. Does that not instill more poverty because the child may not know how to get out of it? It is in a cycle, a condition it has learned, a pattern it is repeating. So, what happens if you remove that piece, and that child, instead of staying in poverty, is given an education, is shown the way? Does that not change the energy of it? Does that not change the outcome or the pattern into which that person has fallen? It changes the momentum.

Think of everything that you do in your life. If you watch TV and you continue to watch it, you start to....well, 'indigestion' would be a good example of that. If you have that and you keep seeing it, eventually you will create it. What it means is to remove human condition, human filters, is to become aware and know that every time you recognize one, you don't accept it. "I am not accepting that gift. That is not in my reality. I am God realized. I am co-creator. I am made in the image and likeness of. I am the light. I am the sound. I am the momentum. I am unique soul energy."

If you continue to do these things, knowing each step you take, and you do not accept the gift of human condition and what those filters create, what happens to you? You rise up and out of it and soon you become the intention of your life. You become the momentum of the next road. You become the pioneer that is fearless because you know that at every turn there is opportunity.

Q: "G", we talk about all these things that we can do to change. Adults can make those decisions and know to change those thoughts but what about the children that can't do that or don't know that. How can their parents help them?

"G": Children are no different than the adults in the room. They actually are closer to God, closer to God energy than most adults. See, what you think they don't have, they don't. Have they yet learned all the filters that adults have placed upon them? No. They learn them through a series of life events such as when a mother says, "Stop acting so stupid. Quit doing that and acting like a baby. Grow up." You see? "That's just the way it is. The rules are the rules and that's the way it is. I am the boss and you must listen to me." You see these words, these things that you create become a momentum as they go forward.

Someone asked me once, "I have known babies that have come in with cancer or diseases or whatever...?" Well. that is true. Why does that happen? Is it karmic? Absolutely. Is there something that caused it? Yes. Or maybe that child is here to teach the parent a greater lesson in life. Maybe there is something that needs to be resolved or healed in the process. So, don't see it as bad.

Yes, it is heartbreaking to see a child suffer and get sick. But you have to remember, too, that this is still the momentum of choice that the spirit has chosen. Maybe you don't understand because it is a baby, but you know that child had a lifetime before and a lifetime before that and those are a series of karmic events.

When you think about all these things that have happened with children, remember, they learn just by example. They are the greatest watchers of adults, did you know that? You think about a child who sits there and the parent says, "Do as I say but not as I do," yes? Well, are you not setting a momentum for them? So, you see, part of being an adult is to live the example. Rise up and say, "I am fearless"; "there are infinite possibilities to my life"; "nothing can hold me down"; "I can go forward and be anything that I want." What happens to children that are taught that?

Q: "G", say that you put the energy out there because you didn't know any better at the time. How do you repair that relationship with your children? Perhaps they are dead or even in another state and are not talking to you anymore?

"G": Part of it is that it's more for you to heal this, not for them. Even though you want it bad enough, part of it is to forgive yourself for the journey, for the wrong choices that you think you made. But you have to remember, there really is no wrong. There is only a series of opportunities to learn, to expand, and to grow.

What I always tell the students that come to me, the masters that I am teaching on the road, is that they must write a letter of forgiveness to themselves. Write a letter of forgiveness and tell the child how you feel. I am not telling you to send it. I am telling you not to go that road and send it because maybe they are not ready to hear it. But just the act of doing it and letting it go to God or letting it go to Infinite energy begins the cycle of repairing the moment.

You must learn to forgive yourself for the mistakes

that you believe you have made and realize that a mistake is only a choice that you may have made that wasn't quite right at the time.

Q: "G", can you explain the dynamics of Infinite energy?

"G": Absolutely. Think about all that is, creation, God. That is Infinite energy. It is all in existence. Everything that has ever been is in it. One of the most amazing things that I have come to understand is that if mankind embraced unconditional love, if every human, every living organism in the entire universe, every master in the heavens, every angel that is, were to hold unconditional love, the whole of that would not fit into the all of God. It would be bigger. So, think about how powerful that can be and how it would expand the All. It would be beyond what All is. It would be like transforming the All of existence.

Q: How would we get from mundane energy to Infinite energy?

"G": Mundane energy is that suppressed spirit. It's caught up in the thing that keeps happening over and over, that play you keep repeating over and over in your head. To find Infinite energy is to stop that cycle.

You know how you can play a CD and put it on repeat and it plays and it plays and it plays until your head is spinning? Well, let me tell you something. STOP! Hit 'stop'! That's the one thing you've got to do first, hit the stop button. Once you do that, you can sit there and go "ahhh". So stop. And when you stop that from going, what's the next thing you can do?

Recognize the pattern in which you are cycling and, once you recognize it, that is 'stopping the roll', you see? The roll, that's like letting go. You say, "Ok, God, Ok

Infinite energy. I think I realize what I've been doing. I recognize the cycle and I think I need to do something about it."

Then I say, "Stop, drop, and roll." You see? Stop...DROP. So you've got this thing, you go, "Here it is, here it is, here it is. I've got this big old condition, "G". I've got this big old condition. What am I supposed to do with it?" And I say, turn it over to God. Turn it over to Infinite energy and say "I'm giving this to you because I am releasing it so that I can now move to the next level of my own awareness, the next level of my conscious awareness, so that I'm not walking in that state of a 'living dead' person." When I say 'living dead' it's like zombies walking the street. You are no longer there because you are conscious, aware, and you start recognizing when you make a mistake. "Oh, I need to correct that." It is done.

When you are walking in your life and you see you have a pattern going, you say, "Oh, that is a pattern and I need to change it." See, I truly believe that the greatest teacher you have is you and each other because you look at each other all the time.

Think about the person who sits across the room from you. "Oh, yeah, that's a mirror to me. I can see that, hmmhmm. I can see that. Oh. So, why is this person doing this to me? Why is this person sending me those dirty looks? What is that?" Well, what it may be is the fact that you are giving her dirty looks across the room.

So, you see, you have to start being aware of everything you do. You cannot walk unconscious in life. And that's when you think, "Well, it was my subconscious. I didn't know any better." Pfftt. Yes, you did. It's not like you can go through life without your foot knowing that it has to go right or left. Your foot will only go where you send it. So is it subconscious? No.

Q: So, is energy always reflecting back what I am sending out?

"G": Yes. I will tell you why. There is always something coming at you. You know how you hear people say, "Well, "G", is this for me or is this for someone else?" There is always an exchange, no matter what it is. Even if you were watching a series of events happen, like seeing something in slow motion. You know, like you're sitting there and they do that really slow motion where you see the guy running really slow and you go, "wow." And you actually see how he does that somersault as he rolls down and lands on his feet? Well, if you had not seen that in slow motion, would you have known how he did it? So think of it like that.

When something comes at you, it may not be personally directed at you but you learn. You say, "Oh, did you see how he did that? I've got to remember that." So you see, it may be coming at you, it may not be a lesson for you, but it might be something that you can use later on.

Everything that comes at you is a teaching tool. Everything that comes at you is an opportunity to expand. So, when it comes at you, it doesn't always mean it is a consequence of some bad event. Maybe what it does is it is just showing itself so you can say, "mental/spiritual note;" mental - hold it in the holding cell so you can tap in spiritually to get it next time, you see. And your spirit says, "Yes, we'll keep that in the memory banks so that next time we see something happen like that, we know."

Think about a small child – I love this story. The little boy was watching, I believe, a show called 911. It was on TV and the little boy sat and watched the story about a mother who had had a diabetic reaction. The little boy watched the TV set and was very little, three years old. But he watched the show and all of a sudden his mother fell down and lay on the floor and he remembered that he was supposed to pick up the phone and push 911 because they showed it on TV. That little boy remembered it.

That came at him, not because it was something bad, but it was something that he could use later on like a series of information. The little boy dialed 911 and the operator asked, "How old are you?" He said, "Free." And she asked, "What's the matter?" And he says, "My mama is laying on the floor. She can't get up." They sent an ambulance over. The mother would have died if the little boy had not remembered.

So think about when you see someone doing something. It may not be directed at you. It may not be some huge lesson that you have to learn, but remember everything that you experience is an opportunity to improve, to grow, to expand, and to utilize your unique soul energy to its maximum height and that's God realized.

Q: "G", how can I see everything as good?

"G": The first thing you have to do is get emotion out of the way. Think about emotion. It can be your friend or your enemy. Do you know how? Emotion gives you the ability to create what you want because it is very powerful. Emotion is very powerful. There are ways of controlling the energy of emotion.

Think about sympathy and empathy. Sympathy, when it is projected on someone who is having a bad day creates an energy of more chaos, more problems. But if you send that same emotional energy with empathy to them, you have changed the vibration of that emotion. All of a sudden you are no longer feeding the chaos. You are calming the sea.

Because you are no longer emotional in the sense that you are creating more havoc you are coming at it with an objective view that says, "I now see this not in the middle of spinning with the person, but from outside looking in, seeing where I can help that person to recognize within themselves, to help guide them." That is how you can do it. It is very good because, you see, emotion is not your enemy. It's just the use of it.

Everything comes down to how you use Infinite energy. There is no good or bad. It's just thinking about what you are doing with it. When you are using Infinite energy, you are in love, love, love, love and you are so good. Everything is so happy and you go through life. You would not want to hurt a single soul because you are walking in unconditional love. But the moment that you remove yourself from it and start not using Infinite energy in a positive way, but using *you* like through the mind, that filter of the mind, think about how much havoc it has created for you. Think of how much chaos you have created out of your sense of your mind – a lot.

Q: "G", as we are learning about the energy and becoming more aware of this energy and that it is our birthright given to us to co-create with God, we now need to become very responsible in our use of this energy. Correct?

"G": Correct. Because you see, you are a co-creator in the journey. God cannot live your life. He cannot choose for you. That was given to you at birth. It said the moment of your uniqueness when you became aware of you, you were granted choice. You were granted free will. So, now the spirit says, "I have spirit's will. I can do this." And it went out into the world.

So you see, the accountability of the journey now is to take hold of your life. Don't become the victim of your journey. Do not let your life succumb to you. Do not let your life suppress you. Let your life be what rises you up, lifts you up. Everything that you do in life, every response that you have, has an impact on your life whether it is you, other people, or the earth. Do you not interact with each other; do you not say words that hurt people? I am not saying that you are responsible for that person taking it on, but there is still accountability to the word said.

Think about this, when you say something to someone like yell at them or be angry at that person, whoever it may be, and that person never truly accepts the gift of your life, all of a sudden, what happens to the gift? Is not that person forced to keep it? Yes. I heard a poet once say, "When you give love and you send it out and it is not received, love returns to soften the road." Think about that same analogy when you send out anger, rage, or sadness. Is it not going to come back to the exact original point of origin? That is why I say, remember what you send forth in the energy of your life, for in that energy, it will return greater fold than what you sent. They call it "G" fold. I call it "G" force. Think of the impact of energy when it is sent out with such a fury, what happens? It comes back to you.

Q: If all of our words, thoughts, feelings and emotions are so powerful and have such an effect on things, how does that affect the earth?

"G": Your earth is energy too, just like you are. Think about when you send anger to the earth or rage or you have fear or you think it's the end. I have told you again, and again, and again in these last few sessions, your words create. So, if you have a fear that this planet cannot support you, what will the Universe bring to you? A planet that cannot support you.

That is why I am telling you to mind your words. Watch what you say because the very words you speak become the action and the truth of your life. If you believe that this planet is going through global warming and will eventually not be able to sustain life or you say, "it cannot be reversed," guess what? It cannot be reversed.

Man is evolving because the involution inside, what is going on inside truly impacts the outer evolution of his life. When you think about your life in this journey, ask yourself, "Am I speaking the words of truth and light or am I speaking the words of fear and doubt?" In this moment of your journey when you think about where you are going, remember that energy is continually moving and continually going, and you are continually moving and continually growing.

This is the only life right now that you have. You cannot touch the future because it is not yours to touch. The past is done, so to speak, if you think of the timeline that man has created. What you can do is live this life with such energy and power that as you create in your world, your world becomes the reflection of your beauty. If man stands in unconditional love and it can outshine all of existence, would not this planet be all beautiful and all whole, just like all of you?

It's time to go forward in life, not falling into fear or doubt or indecision or uncertainty, but to move through these series of things and create the dynamic energy that you are. You see, God does not make crap. God makes perfection. That's what you must hold inside this spirit, because the energy of that perfection is the reflection that you will have in your life.

Q: How would one know what perfection is since it is different for everyone?

"G": Think of it like this. God is not looking for perfection, He already knows it. He sees it in all of you. You are the ones that hold imperfection. You are the ones that see your failures or mistakes. A master who walks in life does not walk in perfection. What he does is, he walks in life recognizing his imperfections and moves to correct them or moves forward achieving perfection.

Think about all the things that are around you, all the different things that have happened in your life, yes? Have you not made mistakes, have you not fallen down, have you not made wrong choices? But have you not also corrected all of them or are in the process of correcting all of them? So, you see, it is just a series of events.

First you have to recognize it, then you have to figure out what you need to do next, and finally there comes a point…..somebody asked "G" once a long time ago, "If one reaches perfection, "G", does that mean you go to the light and that's it?" And I laughed and said, "Well, you're already perfection. You know you're just kind of going through this whole psychological cloud that says you're not." And they went, "Oh."

But really, in all these things that are happening, you live in this veil, in this hidden world inside you. I know what your perfection is. I see the beauty of you. The one thing that mankind has to hold for all is hope, because the moment you lose hope, you are in trouble. You must be very grateful and very thankful for the journey because it teaches you many things. The one thing you must remember, God holds divine hope, and thank God that He does. Because what if He didn't?

Intention

When the moment of truth was revealed
I began to see that I hovered between
Fear of my own lack and the power of joyous enlightenment.
I began to feel the sacred heart
And I now know that this moment, I have a choice.
I know in this very moment
That I am God in action.

There came a time in my journey when all this seemed so huge that I did not believe I could go the road. I felt the pull of non-productive emotion. I truly believed this was all bull-shit, but the interesting thing, is that even though I tried to go back to my old way of life, I found that I couldn't unknow what I know. And, I realized that I really did not like that person anymore.

I became aware that I could not stay there in the old. Every time I went back, I realized another reason why I wanted a different life. It's amazing how the spirit, when it is recognized and set free, can never really return to the old way of life. When I did try to go back, I found myself deeper into depression and chaos.

I know that if I had stayed in that familiar place of non-productive emotion, I would have gotten lost in the world that I had so desperately been running from. I am thankful that I have such wonderful friends and colleagues that stand by me, and believe in me and the journey we are all walking together. I believe that because they stayed close to me and held the light of God so that I could see the light, it revealed to me that what I had been doing was hovering between the choice to stay lost in the grayness of my life and claiming the amazing life that says I am the true intention of the journey now.

This was a very interesting part of the journey because it happened during the writing of this book. I had held the belief that I would never make it as a writer and teacher. I continually fought the idea of being published. Then one day I realized that if I couldn't live the words I teach, I would never go the distance of the journey because I would be in constant conflict. And at some point in the road, it would have come to a head. So instead, I am living the truth of this journey now.

What do I mean by that? Well, my whole life is an intention and I am the outcome of the road walked. We have to get back to that place of claiming our life and knowing we are that creation in action. I know without a doubt that we are the most powerful beings on earth and we are the product of our own life. This road is about us – you and me.

What is intention? What is the use of intention? How do we command it? What is the difference between responsibility and accountability? What is my connection to it? Are there different intentions? Does everything we do have an intention? These are some of the questions that I will answer in this section of the book to help clarify the intention of the journey.

What Is Intention?

Intention is our use of God energy. It is behind everything we say, think, feel, emote or do. Our entire life is an intention. Remember, everything has a destination and that destination is the direction we choose to go.

Think of our life and the places that we have traveled. Now, we must realize that we only go where we choose to go. There is no one out there, nor any other energy, that is making us do things without our permission. Our life is not an accident waiting to happen. We put forth everything in our life. I know this is something that we have all heard before - that we must watch our words and what we say and do. The catch is that we really do nothing to truly change the momentum of our lives. You see, this would mean that we would actually have to take accountability for them.

Here it is folks. We are the reason that our life is out of control. I remember that road well. I truly believed that I knew what was causing my life to feel so unsatisfying. I did not want to see that I was the reason my life was the way it was. I could not possibly be the cause and the effect of my whole life, could I?

I know that at some point I was all about blame. "Did you see what that S.O.B. did to me? It's his fault that my entire life sucks. If he hadn't shown up in my life and lived in my house, sucking the very life from me, living off me while I supported him and never saying a damn word of thanks, then I wouldn't be here in this mess."

Sound familiar? Or maybe, it was my responsibility to take care of him and the world, so what am I supposed to do? Oh heck, why not play the whole victim role? That's my personal favorite. That's the one I played for years. "You just don't understand. My life is hard and I just seem to get deeper and deeper into debt. When I think I am about to get ahead, something always happens to screw it up. This must be my lot in life - to suffer. I just don't see any way out."

Hey, I even used the words, "I think positive all the time and I still get this shit." What I didn't realize was that *every* word, *every* thought, *every* feeling, *every* emotion, and *every* action had a personal outcome. We tend to forget that this is about staying on top of everything that we do.

Before I go any further, I would like to add that every person has a different story to tell. We need to remember that this is only an example of things I have heard. I am sharing this to help people see how we all interpret things differently based on our own personal experiences. This is not to say that there is only one side to a story. Actually, there can be multiple views of the same event. So the use of these stories is to show how we get into blame and not take accountability for our part in a relationship.

What Is The Use Of Intention And How Do I Command It?

Conscious use of energy (CUE) is directing the God energy or intention. CUE is a clue to us, to help us see what we're creating and the direction we're going with that creation.

The CUE of intention is to create everything in our lives. What I am saying is that intention is ambiguous at first because there is no real focus to it. The words we say, the thoughts we think, the feelings we have, and the emotions that we put forward in our lives are the force behind creating with intention. In fact, anything we give priority to is an intention in our journey.

Think of God as this endless supply of energy. We are given an opportunity to use this endless power of Source to create within our life. It is also a continuous chance to redefine our life when we have misused the God energy. When we do not use our power of intention for our highest good, it creates problems on our path.

The use of intention is a meeting point for God energy and connects the power of words, thoughts, feelings, and emotions into a joint creation with God. To learn this piece is to help people achieve everything they desire in their life.

Someone once asked "G" what happens if you have misused this intention? What can we do to correct it? "G" said, *"When you discover that you have created something you feel is not in your highest good, look at the triggers, patterns and old tapes that spurred that creation. A trigger is anything you have learned, such as an old belief that obesity runs in the family. An old tape is something you replay in your head or say over and over again such as "I just look at food and I gain weight." A pattern is something you have seen happen over and over again, and you expect it to happen again. An example of a pattern could be a fear that you are carrying in your mind that you will die of obesity because your father and grandmother did."*

When we discover these triggers, old tapes and patterns, it can feel like we will never be able to overcome them. Well, I'm breaking the news to you. We can overcome them.

The first thing we need to do is to recognize what issues we have given our power to. That's what we did when we discovered the triggers, old tapes and patterns mentioned above. Then replace them with new thoughts, new words. Create a proclamation like "I proclaim I have perfect health." "I am my perfect size, and perfect weight, and everything that I take into this body is for my highest good and with great ease." Whether or not this will be effective falls on how much faith we have in us. The more faith we have, the easier it is to change them.

If we believe we don't have enough faith, then I suggest getting assistance from others. Some of my students created a healing prayer network to help other people with difficult problems that feel too big for them to release on their own. When people are so bogged down with fear it can be helpful in assisting them to release these issues to God. A healing prayer network can be found in many community churches as well as spiritual centers in most areas of the country. God energy is not picky about who holds the prayer. It just needs to be held by someone who is not emotionally attached to the issue(s). God sees everything as good.

Remember that we are not alone and that God is unconditional love. This Source light of creation, God energy, desires for us to have it all. So we must go back and reclaim our whole life.

When we begin to believe in this new momentum, in this new us, we will see changes in our lives. Knowing that we have help and that we can keep redefining the journey, helps us to retrain the mind and begin a new way of living. This begins with our personal power of creation and focusing the energy toward a specific outcome. Every thought is focused to some level. Even when we think randomly, we are using intention though we are unaware of its use and impact. When we focus repeatedly on a thought, it becomes a pattern that we begin to repeat. We start to recognize the things that are happening.

To truly use intention is to be open to the fact that it is a birthright. We are continually moving toward a greater understanding of who we are and the reason why we all signed up for this mission in the first place. That knowledge makes it easier to go the road and heal the whole planet.

We are unique and special, and this means that we are the individualized part of the journey. We are continually moving and have to become that intention that we command. It is our birthright to be present and in the driver's seat of our unique soul energy. What this means is intention is at our command, patiently waiting for the moment that we create. We must realize that when we are commanding the energy of intention, we are determining the use of it and it is important that we remain accountable to ourselves and our lives. We loose the ability to command intention when we're holding on to the responsibility for others.

What Is The Difference Between Responsibility And Accountability?

Part of this journey is recognizing accountability versus responsibility. Responsibility is everything external. It is taking care of our children, our job, our homes. Responsibility is all those things we don't have control over, but we seem to think that we do. Think of our children, our spouses. Can we control them? Can we make them do anything? We are not responsible for them because they have a choice.

Accountability is internal. That is where we are accountable to ourselves for what we say, what we do, and how we act. It is all of our words, thoughts, feelings and emotions. CUE is accountability.

Most of the time we fall into the role of responsibility out of sensibility, which in other words, means doing something out of obligation, guilt, or feeling bad for someone or something. What happens is that responsibility kicks in when we think it's our job or obligation to fix the person or situation. We tend to feel responsible for everything and everyone because we are taught that we must put others first our entire life. The moment that we think of honoring ourselves, we are told that it is being selfish. We seem to forget that we cannot fix anyone but ourselves. We are only accountable for our personal space and everything within it. That is us.

When we are in relationships with people and we're sitting there with family or friends and we say, "I feel really bad for you," what does that do? We are trying to take responsibility and make it accountability because we are feeling responsible for how they are feeling. We are also creating karma between the two of us. We are not in empathy; We're in sympathy.

If we are only accountable for ourselves, then why do we keep falling back into responsibility? Because it is easier to manage things outside of self than inside of self. See, responsibility is familiar. Can we manage someone else? No. But we try. Say we are a director responsible for 100 employees. In this case, what are we really responsible for? The department's goals and showing employees their own accountability. How do we show them accountability? We have to become the words we speak. If we are not reliable or trustworthy, if we fail to do our part in the microcosm of things, what happens? We have exemplified not being accountable so they aren't accountable either.

Does accountability mean we don't need to provide for our family, take care of our children, etc? No. When we care about someone and desire to do something for them, when we are accountable, we are doing it out of love not out of a sense of duty. This intention helps us to define what responsibility is and accountability is as it pertains to others.

What Is My Connection To Intention?

Our connection to intention is all that we are because we have intention in every moment of every day, whether we realize it or not. The everything of us is our life, journey, road, outcome, and excuse. We are the reason that our life is as it is. When we truly connect to our true intention then we are the co in co-creation.

We tend to sit back trying to be oblivious to our part of the journey because if we take accountability, we no longer have someone or something to blame. There is nothing more to focus on other than self. It is our accountability for our life that we must recognize as the connection to our direct part of intention.

Many times we lose the understanding of our direction in intention because we cycle in and out of our life, thinking we are not connected to God. We have to understand that we can never really be disconnected because we are symbiant to God. We are the true witness of God, to see all that is before us. Creation with God is the beautiful light that we tend to ignore.

Are There Different Intentions?

There are three types of intention: random, focused and true.

The first of the three is *random intention*. Random intention is an unfocused thought, such as a fleeting thought in our minds. It just goes wherever it is. It's not something we deliberately go after. We're unaware of it. They also include old tapes we play in our heads like, "God, I'm stupid." "I look so fat. I feel fat." "I'm such a loser."

With random intention, we're in that pattern of reacting. It is an external reaction to an external world.

Random patterns are old patterns we're unaware of. An example of a random pattern would be always picking the same type of man in relationships so that each relationship fails.

Habits are developed as a result of old patterns and can include cigarette smoking, drinking alcohol, lying, being late. We are aware that we do these things, but we don't always know why we do them. That is why they are considered random intention.

Random intention is usually triggered by emotion. For example, stress is an external factor we allow in as a random emotion that causes us to smoke, drink or do something to relieve the stress. For example, I was so miserable in my relationship that when I came home, I would sit in my truck outside my house for hours talking on the phone to avoid going into the house. I thought I was in the truck just making calls when, in reality, I didn't realize I was sitting there to avoid my husband and the way he treated me when I came home. I was reacting externally to an internal situation. The random intention was to avoid my husband when I thought I was just making calls. Had I been aware that my intention was to avoid my husband rather than make phone calls, it would have been an example of focused intention rather than random intention.

Focused intention is our internal response to the external world. A response is different from a reaction in that when we respond, we are aware of our thoughts, words, feelings and emotions; whereas, when we react in random intention we are not aware of them. Responding is focused because we know exactly where we're going with it. Responding is not based on the external anymore. It's based more internally. Random intention, or reaction, drives us rather than us driving them. When we add focused intention to thoughts, words, feelings and emotions, we are sending deliberate thoughts, words, feelings and emotions towards something. We are driving them.

Focused can be emotional, but it's advised that when we are making decisions, we do not do so based on an emotional feeling because most of the time when we do, it's not in our highest good.

In focused intention, our spirit or master higher self can connect and use the third type of intention, *true intention*. It is the God energy or God in motion. It is the internal, indwelling God within, the God inside us. True intention comes from a place of knowing.

True intention is used with random and focused intention. With true intention, it is where enlightenment begins to take hold. We begin to recognize the things we're doing and the patterns we're creating. We start changing them faster and faster until we're no longer in that place of suspension of thoughts. Rather we are conscious and aware at every moment that we are creating with this energy. Think of true intention as the momentum of God energy.

When we are in true intention, we don't take on the emotion in non-productive situations. Focused intention can be misused because it is God energy and the co-creation. God loves us and will grant whatever we put forth in our road because he doesn't discriminate. True intention is the true use of God energy. Focused intention is our tool to use with true intention.

When we are being deliberate about what we create, we have to be very conscious and forthright in what we truly want in this journey because if we aren't, we will continue to misuse true intention or God energy. The result is chaos. I have learned that one well. I used to sit there and say my words created and I'd go out, watch my words, but not watch my thoughts. So my words said one thing and my thoughts another. Then my thoughts began to create and I became a conflict in my own life.

I kept thinking, "This must be God's will. I'm saying all these positive words," but my mind kept going back to a failed relationship, a foreclosed house. My words said that "I get to keep my house now. My house is mine. I have all the money I need to share and spare." But my thoughts would run back to "I have no money. Where are we going to get the money? What the hell am I doing?" Fear, fear, fear.

So God, true intention, had to grant me exactly the contradiction in my mind. Even though I was saying the words, my emotions were still matched to fear and the fear of losing my house to foreclosure was granted to me. I may have been saying the right words. I may have been talking the talk, but I wasn't walking the talk. We really need to do both in order for it to work. I was falling short and allowing old tapes and old patterns and old habits to take over. I truly wasn't "acting as if".

Sometimes when we have a difficult time letting go of something, or truly believing in it because it seems too big a stretch, just to help us move past it, we have to "act as if" we believe it. God sees the action of "acting as if" as real because all God sees is our intention. Even if it's a struggle to keep going, and we just keep acting as if, we will get what we desire because eventually we become exactly what we set out to be or get in our life. It becomes a focused intention and the outcome of our life.

To elaborate further on the foreclosure example above, when I was a young child, I had heard my grandmother say that my father "always pissed money away. He never knew how to manage it and that's why they're always in financial trouble. Let's just hope it doesn't rub off on the girls." I had forgotten about those words all those years ago. Then, while I was in the midst of losing my house, I heard my grandmother tell my mother, "Victor could never manage money. Believe it or not, it rubbed off on the girls." Hearing those words caused me to remember the words I had heard so long ago as a child. I realized those words had stayed with me when I initially heard them and I had allowed them to create losing the house to foreclosure.

In this example, the random intentions were affecting my focused intentions because I still was holding to old patterns, old tapes and old beliefs. Now, my husband had his own lack issues that contributed to this, but we will only discuss my accountability in this example. I had to become aware and admit to myself that I desired to have a new focus, a new pattern and a new direction to what I was focusing on in my life. I began to use focused intention to address the financial hardship and create new patterns. The old patterns were making late payments, not making payments at all and saying, "I'll never own a new car." I now make payments all the time and they are on time. I changed the way I thought about bills and money. I give thanks for everything I pay for. I also changed the negative statement about a new car to, "I have a new car now." With that intention, I added to it the focus that I'd have the money to pay for that car. Then I visualized, also with focused intention, paying my bills on time every month. True intention fulfilled those thoughts, words, feelings and emotions and today I own a beautiful, fully loaded, brand new truck that I have always desired.

Part of the healing process is admitting these things because until we recognize them, things won't change. That was the only way I could truly move into an enlightened place of allowing my master higher self to come in, quieting the old and replacing it with new. This is where true intention can really be directed. We become the conductor of the God energy, the true intention now. As a result, I feel a strong need to go back over my life with a fine tooth comb to see what other dust bunnies I can find under my bed!

Channeling by "G"
"Intention"

Note: The following text is transcribed from an actual channeling by "G". The content and grammar is written as spoken by "G".

"G": Hello, this is "G". Tonight's segment is on intention, the different reasons why you go forward in life, the intention and the purpose of the use of energy and why you claim your birthright in this journey. To understand this journey, you have to come to the realization that you are the intention of your life. That is how you become God realized.

"G": Hello, everyone.
All: Hello, "G".
"G": And how are all of you?
All: Very well.

"G": Tonight we are going to talk about intention and the different levels that there are. In the last segment, I discussed energy and how energy is the use of intention. When you think about energy and you think about all the different types of energy that are out there, the ones that you need to recognize are the ones I talked about: Source or Infinite energy which we call God energy, spirit energy which is your divine spirit, mind energy which is the direction in which you think, thoughts, and all that kind of stuff, and then in the last part we talk about unique soul energy. That is the coming together of all the other energies to make form which makes all of you. So, in this part, we talk about how your unique soul energy uses intention to create and direct your life.

Q: "G", would you please clarify for me exactly what you mean by intention?

"G": Absolutely. Intention is your use of God energy; it is the use of it, by your thoughts, words, feelings, emotions and the direction in which you put them. Think about that. Your intention in life is what you put out in your life. Correct? Think about where you are going in your life. Your life doesn't just sit there and float around... well it can, but it's kind of hard to do that because energy is always moving, but you see, even though you think there is nothing going on in your intention, it is always going on, all the time. So when you sit there and think about intention, thoughts go out to the universe. There is an intention to it. Even those little thoughts that you don't think mean anything, fleeting at best because you let go of that thought, as fleeting as it was, it will return to you as an outcome. Those can be the most powerful intentions out there. That's why you can't have just those random thoughts. You must focus your thoughts or they tend to create some not-so-good things. So you see, intention is everything that you do in your life.

Q: So, "G", if we have put something out there and we recognize that we sent it out and would rather change it, how do we do that?

"G": Well, that is a good question because a lot of times when you think about every thought that you have had, it's hard to catch them at first. So "G" created out of a funny little rule I saw man was using, the 30 second rule. I always watch mankind and if they drop food on the floor they quickly blow it off and say "30 second rule", and then eat it as if it never hit the floor. I always thought that was funny. It still fell on the floor and yet you think that if you blow on it, it is still okay to eat it. So I watch you, you blow and you eat it, so you're intention in that is that it didn't really fall on the floor. So I thought, what a great way to give you an out. So what I did was, say "OK, I will give them 30 seconds to change their mind and it's as if they never even said it at all." So, it's like a big giant eraser. You have a big old chalkboard up there in your brain and when you write "I am fat" and then you say, "Oh, 30 second rule" it's like a big old eraser comes along and goes 'whoosh' and it's gone. You see, after I gave this new idea to you, 30 seconds to change your mind, I decided to make it a master number '33 second rule' instead.

Q: So, "G" then as I co-create what is the best intention then to send out my new creation?

"G": Very good. Think of it like what is your highest and greatest accomplishment. You know how you do something in life and how good you feel about it? You think about maybe the birth of a child, how you felt in the moment that the baby was put into your arms, maybe the great promotion you got, or maybe something amazing that happened in your life. You know how that feels, yes? Well that is energy and that energy is very powerful so if you think about what you create with…if you create with joy and happiness and love, the energy of intention says "so it will be" and all of a sudden you create all of these beautiful things in your life because you are emulating the very light that you have so desired. Now if you go with the negative like fear, doubt, all those things that make you feel bad, the intention of energy says it must be and it goes and creates exactly what is sent out and it hears.

Q: You said energy uses intention, correct? Does intention use energy?

"G": Absolutely. It's a two way street folks. One can't be without the other. Like you can't be without God, and God can't be without you. That is how it works. It is all symbiant.

Q: "G", which intention has the greatest momentum and how many levels of intention are there?

"G": Very good, very good. Well there are many levels of intention, but what we will discuss are the three highest intentions because those are the ones that you have the greatest impact on. There is true intention which is the use of God light energy and the focus of light. True intention is the highest level and it is all good.

Random intention is the one we misuse; it is unfocused use of intention. It's like random thoughts; things that you just let go of and forget about and then all of a sudden that random thought pops up in your life.

Then there is the use of focused intention. Think about what you focus on in your life. That means you know exactly what and where you are going to use this God energy. It's not just sitting there idle. It doesn't go idle, but moving and holding to whatever you are putting out there. It really is about putting it in the direction you desire.

Random intention is either the misuse of intention, unfocused intention, or the misuse of God energy. See, it's still going, folks. Even if you don't realize it, it has to deliver to you. Even when you sit not making a decision, guess what? That is making the decision to wait. See, people sit there and say "Well, I will just wait". Well, you can't wait. Waiting doesn't work because when you are waiting, you're really not waiting. Think about that. A decision is made even when you are thinking you are waiting about making a decision.

So, think about the random misuse of intention. I bet everyone in this room can probably mention something today that has happened in their life. Think about that, just today when you woke up and put your foot down on the floor and you went "Ow, pain, I've got pain. Why do I have pain?" Now, with focused intention, you immediately would have recognized that it was a signal and you immediately would do everything you could to alleviate it; you would meditate, turn it over to God, do all the things that you need to do to let go. Correct? But what do you do most of the time? "Oh no, why does my foot hurt? There has to be a reason behind it. Why am I feeling this?"

Q: "G", you mentioned that I could turn it over to God. Could you explain that a little bit more to me, please?

"G": Absolutely. Your greatest power is the fact that you are made in the image and likeness of God and that you are a co-creator with God. When you are feeling pain, when you are emotional or out of sorts, that means that you are the furthest away from God. See, what you have to do is come back. Meditation brings you back. Sending healing energy to the spot sends you back. It puts you back into your own driver's seat instead of letting the pain be the factor in it. Pain is random. Have you ever noticed that? Well, that random pain, guess what? It is a signal. That is not the issue. It's a signal. It's telling you that there is a misuse of energy and that what you have to do is come back to that place and say "Obviously there is a misuse of energy in this space" and you need to redirect the signal to the body that says "I am healed, whole and complete." And by the power of you, because you are a co-creator, you command it.

Now I know you say "Well "G" I understand that, but when I step down on it, I still feel pain." You need to remind yourself over and over and over again, "No, I am letting this go." It is a reminder to get you stronger in your knowing.

Q: So, when we have a pain, that is obviously something very easy to identify. It's easy to focus our mind on that. You just stated that it is a random issue that is taking place. Many of us here may tend to think much of our day we are in focused intention, but what I'm hearing from you is, we probably aren't.

"G": Absolutely not. Most humans tend to wander around and be pretty clueless about life. Your thoughts are usually somewhere else, not present here in the moment. You are usually off thinking about yesterday or thinking about the kids or thinking about dinner or thinking about this or that. Correct? And when your mind is not present, what do you think happens? You do stupid stuff, sometimes. You stub your toe because you're not paying attention to where you're walking. You focus on the things that are not really that vital. Here's the thing: What happens if you are not focused in what you know, if you are not consciously alive in your life, directing your thoughts, directing your words, directing all that is you? Your life will run away without you, so to speak. It's like you're along for the ride, but not the one driving it. Isn't that funny? How many times have you, all of a sudden, heard someone cough and your thoughts go "Oh no ". Think about the cold. I was talking about that in an earlier segment. You think about that cold, just think about a cold. What comes to your mind when you think about it? And you've got TV going, "Cold season. Get your flu shot right away. You might need it. Here, it's happening at these places. Come get your flu shot." Well, you know what? That tells the Universe that you're worried about getting the flu, getting the cold. And guess what? You get a cold. It's just a matter of time. Obviously there is a moment when you finally let it go. If you say '33 second rule' when you think about it, then it is gone, but you see, how many in this room really have done that? You just learned about it, right? So, the intention now is to direct it. Instead of letting your mind go where it doesn't need to go, you now are learning how to direct it by using things like "33 second rule". The other one, the release statement, I talked about in other segments also:

""G", anything I may have said, spoken ill, thought, felt, emoted, or did that is contrary to my highest good, anything suppressed, repressed, suspended, or hanging around that is contrary to my highest good, I release it all to you now for my highest good and with great ease."

Those are the two things that you can use to help you not get caught up in random or unfocused intention. Most people usually say, "Wow, "G" that was the best thing you could have done because every time I do it, it's gone. It doesn't happen. It's like it gets rid of it." The reason that it works is because you have created it out of food falling on the floor and your faith in the rules. With this direction, the focused intention is where you need to be in order to help yourselves.

Q: So, just for some clarity, "G", if, when I get up in the morning, I step and go "Ow", a way to redirect that random intention is to see that this is my spirit, my energy, the universe, reminding me to focus my energy?

"G": Yes, you have to be present. See, you may have forgotten about the things that you were thinking about when you went to bed.   Now you have just woke up and you're pretty sleepy. "Oh, I could sleep another hour "G", that would be really good." But when you get up, yes, at times you feel foggy. What is interesting is that man walks in a fog most of the time and when you stub your toe, that is your spirit saying "Attention! Here we are! Focus! Focus! Focus!." And that's what you're to do, recognize it as a reminder to focus, "Thanks for the reminder", "I'm alive, awake, and alert and enthusiastic about my day."

Q: You were talking about pain being random. I can understand that with headaches and if you bang into something, but what about these people that have chronic pain in a particular area?

"G": Well, that's still the same thing. That is still random because they do not believe they have the power to change it. A young woman came to "G", suffering from a human condition called M.S., multiple sclerosis. She was a very sick woman, barely could get up, was very fatigued, achy joints, inflammation, felt terrible, numbness in the arms, having difficulty on one side. There were a lot of things that she was struggling with. She came to "G" and said, ""G", I don't want this anymore. What can I do?" And I said, "Well, first things first, quit claiming it. Quit focusing the disease on you. See, when you say "my M.S., my cancer, my, my, my" the Universe says, "Well, it must be for them so I'm going to give it to you." I told her, "The moment you claim it you have put the focus on you and it becomes your focused intention to be sick. It is your focus to have disease or illness or suffering." But see, she came to see "G". Of course it took a while because it meant redirecting her focus, giving her a way to learn to co-create, not claim the disease, say "the disease" or "the M.S.," removing it from her personal being and her personal label. See, it's funny. When you say "my" what does the Universe say? "It's yours." So, it grants it to you. This is why I say to you, folks, all these things that you are going through, all these health issues, all these problems, you know it is all gone. It is an illusion. Think about that for awhile.

Q: "G", how can we hold an intention that impacts our environment and the world?

"G": Well, that's a big one because I can tell you it is very important to do. First things first, we've got to get you focused on self and get yourself out of that before you focus on the world. See, most of the masters that have been sent here to walk this earth are here to guide you to find your self realization. That is what most human beings are going through, discovering self realization. See, most of you don't even know who you are. Most of the time you're just kind of bumping along, stubbing your toe, 'oh, my aching back', 'oh, my darn headache' and not really aware of how much your very own words, thoughts, feelings, and emotions, impact the world. It is vital to have mankind learn to change themselves so that they can stop sending negative energy to their fellow man as well. You know, you do that kind of stuff and your life is whatever is out there. Correct? But you are not directing it; you don't even know who you are. Half the time I hear people say, "Oh, why am I here? What is my purpose in life? I need direction. I need to find myself. I'm on a soul search." Does that sound familiar to you guys in the room here? Yes. So think about that.

Q: People do seem to still have that fixed belief that even to say true intention means that it is something that God has held for us, either as a pre-destination or some idea that God has a will that we need to get into, that is almost separate from us. Could you help me understand how true intention is different?

"G": Absolutely. The difference is that true intention is your spirit, your divine spirit, who you are. We call that spirit's will. That is true intention. I use the word God energy because that is your use of you, the higher level of you, your 'made in image and likeness of', your co-creation piece of God, the part that you are made of and are connected to. So that true intention is really your spirit's will, not your mind's choice, which is the whole part about the mind running rampant and stubbing the toe and not being present or being all somewhere else when you're not here. So, really, it's not God's will or God's destination, it is really your true spirit's will, your higher level self knowing what is for your highest good.

God holds this place of Divine Hope. I see all the good, all the perfection, and all unconditional love. Love, love, love, love is what I hold. So this is where true intention stands. Your use, your spirit's will's use of this intention is really your ability to create the amazing, dynamic life that you all so desperately crave to have. That is really your birthright.

Q: How do I really know what my spirit's will is?

"G": See, there is a way of listening. Your mind is very bright when you are present in your life. Your mind is smart yet your heart is wise. There is heart intelligence in you, and that heart intelligence is your connection to God and your ability to communicate with God. When you need to hear, usually it is that very first impact, that very first thought that comes out that says "YES", but it's the little mind, mind's choice, that goes, "Well, I don't know. We should really think about this. Now are you really sure you want to do that?" See, when you start to question it, that's the little mind trying to take control. The little mind doesn't want to give up its spot. It has been very important for a very long time. Your mind has been the big cheese and all of a sudden man wakes up. Humankind becomes conscious in their life, and they become awake in their journey; they become awake and they say "Oh, this is different when you wake up." The best way to describe the heart is that it's quieter and there is no mind chatter. That's when you know it is your heart communicating. The heart does not have to convince you, it knows what it knows. The mind is always trying to persuade you to the side of doubt.

Q: Backing up just a little bit, you said that spirit's will is connected to true intention. Would it be fair to say then that mind's choice is connected to random intention, or is mind's choice connected to a focused negative intention, or could it be random or focused positive and negative?

"G": Mind's choice is random intention and the misused focused intention. Here is the difference with random intention. Your mind wanders off and just kind of goes places that are fleeting and unfocused, kind of negative, or doesn't really have any direction. You're sitting at your desk, at your computer, running a business and you keep thinking, "Man, the clients are just not calling." That's mind's choice. That's random intention. It's also unfocused intention. Because think about when you sit there for a couple of hours thinking about how the phone isn't ringing. Well, that's a pretty big focus, but it's not conscious.

Random is short bursts, little thoughts that come and go, and they usually are very fast like a snap of the finger. Sometimes you feel like you don't even remember thinking it. But when you get into an unfocused negative thought and you start holding a negative energy, guess what? That little random thought becomes a big old focused intention even if you are not aware it is creating, and guess what happens? It happens to you, like that phone that is not ringing because of the unfocused thought. You must retrain the thoughts and become cognizant of those thoughts.

Now, there is also another part to this. The mind is not in the driver's seat. The mind is a tool. Spirit's will, your spirit, is the real driver and, when put into place, you truly recognize self, self realization. That's when you activate Spirit's will. You become self realized, self sentient, and self aware. All of a sudden you say, "No, I have direction in this. I know exactly what I want to do with this."

When you become aware of your part in the road, your part in the journey, guess what happens? All of a sudden the mind has no other choice, but to quiet because you're not listening to it anymore. You become focused in meditation, start calling in the divine master self, start realizing that the random thoughts that run away with you are really misuse of energy, intention. So, when your mind is doing the talk, what you have to do is bring yourself very present, bring in the master self, the spirit's will. We will talk about master higher self in the segment of the book called *God Realization*.

What you really have to focus on is first recognizing that you're out there, recognizing that it is not just a random thought or unfocused thought anymore, but that it is something that you are thinking. Maybe you are not happy that day, or maybe something happened and you got a little mad at yourself, or you feel that somebody did something that maybe "pissed you off" a little bit. You cannot blame anyone but you, for you're the one driving your car.

You know, it's funny...This is my understanding of the human condition. You have to drive to work. Every day you have to drive to work. Yes? And you get in your car and you sit in your car in rush hour traffic and every day you bitch about being in rush hour traffic. Well, the funny thing I think about the human being is – you know you're already there, you know you gotta go, so why do you bitch every day about going when you know you have to go there anyway? See, to me, that becomes the focused intention and you hear the Universe going "Hmmm, they have been bitching about this every day for two and one-half, or three years because that's how long they have had their job." I see how you keep getting into rush hour traffic, and it's not overnight, but you think traffic has just gotten worse over the years.

The person who becomes aware of spirit's will, who becomes self realized says, "Well, I can create a better traffic flow. I'm conscious and self realized. I know my intention and I am in this journey. I am a co-creator. I have momentum. I am going to create my morning and I'm just going to give it to the heavens. I've done my part of seeing the traffic moving with ease and for my highest good and I'm just going to say 'I am in my day and I'm going forward in my momentum of co-creation'." Guess what happens, folks? It changes. All of a sudden there is no traffic and you go, "People must be on vacation. This is really good." All of a sudden it doesn't matter anymore. The traffic is moving quicker, faster. So, that's what you have to do: be focused in your intention at all times.

Q: If I have a focused intention say to be at work early and I keep having doubts that I am going to get there on time, what is my best way to stay with that momentum of creating a focused intention?

"G": Think of it like this. You have old patterns, correct? You know how you make clothes? I was watching a lady who had this pattern she laid out on top of fabric and she cut it out. Well, she loved this pattern so much that she kept it and she would use it over and over. She loved it so much that when it began to wear out, she would put tape on it when it would tear. This pattern became like plastic she had it for so long. She always liked this pattern because it was so versatile. Just about everything she wore was from this base pattern. "You now this pattern is kind of wearing out. I desire to get a new one." But her doubt says, "Oh, I don't know... you know I'm just never going to find it. This is so old and I'm never going to find another one just like it. I'm just never going to find it." And so she sits there, but she came to hear "G" once, and I was teaching how the power of words, thoughts, feeling, and emotions play a part in you creating what you desire. I said, "Believe it ,even if it is hard. Act as if." I said that God sees all and not the limited view that is mankind's. All of a sudden she says, "You know, I think I'm going to try that whole 'act as if'. I'm going to see if I can direct my life. So the next time she went looking for her favorite pattern, she said, "OK, I found the perfect pattern now."

So as soon as she said it, she let it out, she let it go, but the mind kept running back to that "it's really old, we're talking a good fifteen-year-old pattern, you know." And she would say, "Oh, I don't know." And then she would go "Oh, no, no, no. I'm going to hold this in my spirit's will." So she did this and every time she caught her mind running a different direction she would call it back. Guess what? She went to all the pattern stores, went to all the fabric stores and never found it. She kept holding to that statement about the perfect pattern.

One day she just happened to be driving along and saw a garage sale and decided to stop because she felt her heart was telling her to. "You need to stop at that garage sale." Her thoughts went to the place of, "But I don't like garage sales." "I don't care. You need to stop at that garage sale." She finally listened and said "OK, I'm going to stop at the garage sale." She could not believe what she saw before her: there was row after row of patterns, all kinds of patterns.

She felt like she had been holding her breath. She quickly asked if the woman had her specific pattern. She did and was shocked at how many there were; six patterns are what she found. She had learned that the woman, who once owned all the patterns, was a bit of a pack rat. When she found something she liked she would buy a lot of them. The young woman told her that her mother was now in a nursing home and did not need the extra stuff.

Q: "G", you mentioned she 'acted as if', could you tell me about that?

"G": Absolutely. See, I know human condition. I know humans as a whole have a difficult time holding things to a positive, when all around them are negative things, such as an old pattern that you keep repeating like, "Oh, there I go again." See, sometimes when you have a difficult time letting go of something, or truly believing in it, it seems too big a stretch, just to help you move past it, you have to act as if you believe it. I had said in earlier segments that God does not deny money. Even if it is counterfeit, God sees it as real, and so if you cannot pray a real prayer, pray anyway. It's all real to God.

God sees the action of 'acting as if' as real. See, you now have to know that it is all real to God and that it is all good. All God sees is the intention of you. Even if it's a struggle to keep going, and you just keep acting as if, you will get what you desire. Say, ""G", I keep acting as if. I'm turning this over to you". Eventually you become exactly what you set out to be or get in your life, because again it becomes a focused intention and the outcome of your life.

Q: Does the same thing happen with prayer?

"G": Yes. Meditation and prayer, it all helps. But see, you don't walk around in a meditative state so it's kind of hard to keep it there but, yes, it's good. You might want to open your day up with meditation. You might want to close your day with a prayer or meditation, but the real 'act as if' is when your mind runs away with itself and takes you back to that place that says 'you're not smart enough' or 'you can't do it'. That's when you need to say "no". You see?

I will give you a perfect example of something like the 'act as if'. It was very interesting, there was a young woman who struggled with drug and alcohol disease for a very long time. She tried to sober many, many times. It was very interesting because everything she did kept bringing her back to her use. Every time she tried to go sober, she just couldn't, and there was a counselor who said to her once, a long time ago, "I'm going to give you something and I want you to listen to me. If you can't do this for you, pick someone and do it for them. Act as if. Do each day as if you are acting the road." And so she did, little by little, step by step. She kept saying "No, I'm doing this. Today I'm doing this. This moment, I'm doing this." Part of the key to acting as if is staying very present, one foot in front of the other. If you can't do it in a day, do it in an hour; if you can't do it in an hour, do it in a minute; if you can't do it in a minute, you do it every second. But it becomes one step after another.

So, that is where you go to this place of 'acting as if'. Eventually she sobered up and it wasn't for the other person. It ended up being for herself. But see she needed to place it off herself because she did not believe she deserved it. She did not believe in her self worth, so she had to pick someone and say "I have to do this for you because I cannot do it for me." But in her sobriety, in the long journey, it finally became for herself.

Q: So, what is it exactly that differentiates between it happening on a negative note versus a good note?

"G": A negative note is because most of the time it's just a thought that runs and it's in a negative state. But, think about it. God is not negative. The intention of true intention is not negative. It is not positive either. It is not defined by good or bad. It just is. Correct? So think about that statement. It's your use of it. Well, one of the things that your higher self knows is that your higher self knows you. So, that is your higher self, the higher knowing, the higher master self that knows you and knows your intention even though you're down here trying to figure your higher self out, finding your self, finding your self realization. This particular part of it is like that soft spot because if you truly look at your life, have you really ever truly hit bottom? No, you haven't.

Think about 'as above, so below'. Have you ever heard that statement? Well, think about a mirror. When you look at something and it mirrors back to you, what is that? That's you, a reflection. Is that not? OK, think about God. If you can't believe that It's tangible, if you can't believe that It's possible, do you see what I'm saying, you will never connect to God. You will never truly have the inner personal relationship with God. It will always be outside of you. It will always be out of reach. And what has happened, because you want that connection to true intention, that true God energy, the use of it, somewhere in all of this, the distance from so far to so far had to come closer together.

The self realized individual recognized their co-creation, misused it, beat themselves up, and removed themselves again from the game. Do you see that? Well see, God watched that. He saw that. You kept going in and out and in and out and you kept doing this so we brought the divine self, the master self closer to you so that now you can merge with that very real spirit's will, that very real God intention. See, it wasn't possible before. Most people had to be pretty advanced on the road to get there.

Now, I gave you co-creation; you got co-creation. Yes? Well, it was great giving it to you but you would create good, create bad, create good, create bad and you were just like a seesaw and a teeter-totter, back and forth, back and forth. What we realized is that we had to get you a little balance. We had to take it to the next level and help man wake up. So what we did was open the door and say it is possible to meet God inside, right here, inside of you. And how it starts is first recognizing your birthright.

And how do you recognize your birthright? Co-creation. Well, you've been doing that, good or bad, good or bad, good or bad. Yes? Then, it's recognizing unconditional love. Yes, it's out there, you've seen it. You might even have had a little bit of feeling of it here and there. And then all of a sudden somebody introduces absolute absolution and you say, "What do you mean I'm forgiven? Before I even did it? That makes no sense." Absolutely it makes sense. But see, you had to come to these places and recognize them and then what happens to you? You recognize all the energy you are using and misusing in life, correct?

Well, now you have come to this place of recognizing the differences between Source, Infinite energy which is God energy, divine spirit energy which is spirit's will, correct? And all of a sudden you move in and you have mind energy – mind's choice. "Oh, here I am, this is me. I am physical." You have physical energy that is walking around going "Oh, I'm here" – unique soul energy – USE. And it is in that USE that says, "I'm unique but yet I am."

The most powerful words that any human being on this planet can use are the words "I AM" for it is the word of creation. "I AM" and whatever follows it becomes so in life. I am health, I am wealth, I am sick, I am poor. It can even be "I have". Do you see what I mean? Anything that follows the word "I", which is God, and "AM", which is you, is the co-creation. "Co" meaning self; "creation" meaning God. But see you kept seeing them as separate. And "G" said, "We recognize this." So, God said, "It is time to bring them closer, to a higher level. They need to feel the God within; they need to recognize the ability to quiet the mind, walk in quiet contemplation, be in the presence of energy, and know that it is their true spirit intention."

Q: "G", I was curious. Is there an external and internal intention?

"G": Very good question. See, most people identify thought, because you're not speaking it, as just in your head thinking. But that in itself is an intention because you're just thinking, thinking, thinking. An external intention is the action by which you do things. Think about the act of something. The act of love is an intention. To strike someone is an intention, do you see that? So internal intention might be the random thoughts that kind of roll around like "Oh, she's so pretty." That's a nice thought, that's a nice internal intention. Somebody gets a car, a nice fancy car, and people see them going by and say "she's got money" or "he's got money." That is an internal intention. So, you see there are many different intentions. It's just how they are perceived or acted upon or even sent out. So, yes, that is a very good question.

Q: "G", in eastern philosophy, people speak about karma. How does karma play a role in focused intention? How can it override focused intention or how can focused intention override karma?

"G": Very good. See, in the earlier segment we talked about energy and we talked about karma. People had asked "what about murder?" It's a mistake and you can't bring the dead person back and someone says, "How can God be forgiving?" or, "How can we just forgive and see this mistake?" See, man creates the very guilt and the very judgment on themselves. If I wrong you, I have to come back and correct the mistake so like I said in the chapter on energy, focused intention is like "I know that I am going to do this to you". Well, that's karma. Good or bad, if you are directing it at someone, it is karma. Now, there is good karma and there is bad karma. Bad karma says that I am going to wrong you. You might steal from someone or you might hurt them in some way. That creates a negative karma between you. But let's say you look at somebody and you love them or send them love or send them flowers. That's karma, but it's a positive karma. It is the focused use, the focused intention, you see, and so you direct it. So, you want good karma? You need to throw out bad karma.

You need to remember, when you are using your true intention, you have to recognize that there is an outcome to it one way or another. Let's say you wrong somebody. How do you rectify that? First there is forgiveness, the act of forgiveness, whether you say to that person you are sorry or you do something to correct the wrong you have done. Maybe it's as simple as forgiving yourself for going there and knowing that you have learned the lesson and will never go there again because you recognize the mistake you have made and you say "I desire good karma." Once you forgive, even if that other person does not forgive you, as long as someone in this relationship forgives and lets go and says, "I will correct this now and let it go" you have cut that karmic loop so you will not have to repeat the pattern in the next lifetime.

Q: With that, I am wondering if you forgive somebody with intention, but they are not aware of it, are you still forgiven?

"G": Very good. You see, real forgiveness has to come from within. If someone else holds a grudge or holds an anger or holds a resentment, that is their journey to choose. Think about a gift. You think about that. If somebody hands you a gift and you don't take it, it does not go anywhere. So, think of it like that when you send the act of forgiveness. Sometimes I have students do legwork and they have to write a forgiveness letter to themselves as the person that they needed forgiveness from, self. And so they did that. Over the years I have heard many, many students say, "It has changed my life, "G". I did not realize how much I held inside of me, how much I felt inside." So, you see, this is part of the learning and the forgiving and the moving forward in your life.

You remember earlier I had talked about true intention and I said the conscious use is really conscious use of energy, CUE. Think of true intention. That is that part where it is God, yes? That is God energy and is your use of God energy. Well, in the truth of this journey, you become conscious and you use the energy. It is your CUE to go forward, you see? So CUE is your cue to use God energy in the right way. You are waking up, all of you. Everyone in this room, everyone on this planet is becoming aware and each time you wake up to the next level of your life, you are alive, you are transformed, you are the conscious birth of your life. This life has to wake up or you will continue to sleep and never really know the real life, the amazing life that is your birthright.

Q: "G", is there any difference between intention and desire?

"G"? Oh, that is very good. See, really there is not. Desire is really holding it in the present, but when you think of want or a need, it keeps it away from you because it is not here. Desire is in the moment. Desire is the intention. Desire says "I desire this" and the true intention goes out and says "All right, I will bring it to you." So, it is the power of focused intention. It is the power of true intention.

Q: Explain a little bit further on want and need. How is that different?

"G": See, want or need is really placing something out of reach. A want says that you can't have because it is wanting, it is beyond, it is far away. A need says desperation. But desire, that is the part that holds the dream. Desire says "I desire this, therefore, I create." Want says "I want what you have," but you don't want what someone else has because to want what someone else has, what is that? To take, correct? You don't want to do that. To need means "I need this to be better, I need this for that." You don't want that either because need says to the Universe "I am desperate." Need implies lack.

You think about "I need monies, I need monies." That's what I hear mankind saying when they call. "I need monies, I need monies." Well, when you say "need" it means you don't have. You want to say "I desire to have all the money to pay my bills and to share and to spare." See, most humans learn to call on God and say, "I need money to pay my bills" or "I desire money to pay my bills," but see you don't go beyond just what you desire. You must see all so that you have all the money to pay, all the money to share, and money to spare. See, you must move to the next level in this. Instead of just getting to that point where you make ends meet, you want to get beyond it, so that you can have all that you desire…an amazing life.

Consciousness, the use of intention, and the energy in which you are using CUE, is what you have to remember. From this point forward, when something comes up, that means you became conscious of it; you became aware of it. Now you are using CUE, the intention of that energy, to change, to move forward, to go the new road of a self realized individual in the journey and finding that place of being in your life.

Now

The secret to life is to be present in it
But I find myself angry at the road.
I was invited to come along
But somehow I fight my very nature
And I ask, "Why?"
I was ordinary and that was fine.
Then I experienced the extraordinary and I was changed.
I no longer could fight what was awakening inside.
And now I sit, wondering about my life.

Now is the moment of truth. This is the space in which we have the greatest impact in our lives. I remember my grandfather telling me that God is everywhere. All we need to do is get quiet and listen. Then we will hear God whispering His secrets to us. If we spend time in the moment, just being, we would truly know God.

You see, my grandfather was an agnostic. He believed that man had confused the true relationship he had with God by telling us we are unworthy of God's love. When He supposedly sent His son to suffer and carry the sins of man, we just filled up space with more unworthiness. My grandfather told me once, "To truly understand the love of God, we need to get to know Him, not with words from a book, but with the feeling in our hearts. That is where we will find Him. It's like the love I have for you. I just love you. It's that simple honey." I never really knew how much that would help me on my journey.

I remember him taking me to different churches as a young girl. He believed there was something out there greater then words could fill. He could see so much with his heart. As a result, many were very intimidated by my grandfather, but not me. I could see right through and past to the real man behind the iron façade.

I have learned from my grandfather that the true place to be is in the present. I know as a spiritual being having a human experience, human experience can pull me out of the moment of now and into the past or the unknown future.

When I think about the road traveled, it always takes me back to the past, or I find myself looking out over the vast unknown future wondering about my life. I really did not see that I hovered between my life and my existence of spirit. They both seemed separate to me. One I lived, the other I wondered about. Yet I've heard others say that their life is the existence of them and they weren't even really aware of their true spirit. Either way the spirit is seen as separate from life. I did not understand that to be present means being accountable to my whole life.

As a result of those experiences with my grandfather, I have to say that I continually looked for a road to walk that would bring me closer to God, so I could really reach out and touch the God I so desperately wanted to know. I kept looking for some sign to prove that God existed. What I realized was that my grandfather was right and the only way to God was to be present in the now and truly walk in my journey as a self realized individual. That means it's not looking for me. It's knowing me. I have finally let go and let

God be really present in my life by creating with the very power he has given me.

Future-Unknown

"G" explained to me that there are three different spaces we live in: the past, the present and the future. While the goal is to always be living in the present, as humans we don't always stay there. We tend to find ourselves in the past and the future more than we'd care to be. But what really is the future? What is the past? And what is the present?

The future holds that unknown space - a place in which we have no tangibles. It's a space of the unfamiliar. It's outside our present space, and when it is outside our space, we believe it's safer to be there.

The future is like that place where God dwells, holding all the infinite possibilities, the billion possible outcomes for any one event. What I mean by that is for any one event in our life on the road we're walking, if we detour just slightly, it creates a different outcome from the one we had been walking.

When they say that God is all-knowing, He is. He is aware of all those possible outcomes. They're not a mystery to God. But to us, they are a mystery because we tend to forget in that space of the unknown that one choice can take us in a completely different direction than the one originally started.

What I find in this journey is that I am the deepest state of being and I continue to move. What is this state I feel? Is it the restlessness of my journey? Am I looking to the end instead of being present in the journey of my life? I believe when we are continually looking for what should be or the what if, then we miss the whole existence of who we are.

The future is not our place, it is God's playground, and we need to leave it that way.

Past-Familiar

When we are afraid to look at the future, some people go to that state of the past. I had heard from spirit that the past was familiar, a place where tangibles exist. It is where we already know the outcome of the journey walked because we have already walked it.

I remember once when I was pretty young. I was with some friends, swimming. It was really interesting because I wasn't the best swimmer at the time, but I was pretty good. Everybody wanted to swim out to this island, and of course, I wrestled with the idea of doing it. I wasn't sure if I had the strength or the ability to swim that far, but I went anyway. The whole time I was thinking, "I can't do this. It's too far, too hard. I've never done this before." Of course I wasn't thinking about what I was saying. At that time, I was unaware that words, thoughts, feelings and emotions create.

Eventually I felt myself beginning to slip under the water because my words were beginning to create my inability to get there. But from my past, I grabbed something that I had heard my grandfather say. "The only sure way to fail is to give up." That memory spurred me on. I pushed myself up and kept thinking, "I can do this." And I swam all the way there.

To me, the past can be a good thing when we remember something that keeps us going. That was the case in this experience. In addition, the past is our history that can help us stop repeating patterns when we're willing to recognize them. The past is that place where we regain a knowing of something.

However, the past can be a problem when it gets misused such as when we are continually worrying that something is going to happen again or when we continually dwell and fall back into old familiar places we have walked that are contrary to our highest good. They are the things that keep us in the negative. When we do this, we don't move forward because when we live in the past, we're continually dwelling in what was and not in what is. We miss the horizon. We don't see it anymore.   It's the past and needs to stay the past.

Because the past is a history, a log of what was that cannot be changed, and the future is the place that holds the infinite possibilities or the billion outcomes that we could pick from, the only place where we can really create is in the now, the present.

Now-Present

The present is the moment. It is right now. It is the place where our life happens.

When we are waiting for something to happen, it is not being in the moment. What I realized was that waiting places us in the past or in the future. If we are waiting for something to happen that "always happens to me", then we are in the past. We are in the future where we are waiting for the unknown to show up.

What's interesting is that we can't wait anymore. We have to be in it, in the game of life. We were all handed a deck of cards at birth. These cards are what we play with in life. What's really nice about playing a deck of cards is if we don't like the cards we were handed, we can toss them out and draw new cards or play another hand.

I remember waking up this morning and what I did was make a promise that this day, I would be conscious and I would set forth with intention all that I needed to do to get my book done, for you see, the book was my priority. What I did was become the manifester of my day, the creator of my moment. I drew from a past memory that pushed me into a place where the more that I put out there with thoughts, the more it took form and became the day. "G" once said, *"I must first accept the moment and rest in the knowing that I am to go inside; that this is where I will find you, me, God."*

I was writing in my journal when it came to me. As the words poured out onto the page, just like in this book, I began to realize that I was with my own God within. I could not have written the words that I have today if I had not been present in the energy of God, the now, the moment, that personal space of God.

What is existence? It is the knowingness of my soul. What is spirit? It is the no-thingness of my soul. What I had to learn was to stop looking outside of me at deadlines, obligations, responsibilities - all those things we're not supposed to be caught up in. The moment that I stopped pushing myself, I became aware that it had been present all along, this God light within, even when I thought it was not.

I asked "G" the question, "What does my soul desire?" He smiled at me and said, *"The answer lies within you."* So, I contemplated the thought and began to see this beautiful crystal bowl in my mind's eye. It was shining and sparkling, but there was nothing inside of the bowl. I was confused, so I asked "G", "Why is the bowl empty?" Then I heard Him say, *"This is God's place to fill and it is your job to keep it in a state of emptiness. No clutter of your life. No mundane thoughts. No ordinary you. For if it is a place of God perfection, the bowl will sing your perfect note."*

I began to see that the existence of self is the knowing of my soul and I found that when I fall into a state of nothingness, I discover the existence of my spirit. The bowl, when filled by God, is my spirit's Oneness with God. So, I embraced this place in my journey, for I learned that everything in me is extraordinary. I am the one that had to take a chance in my life and be present in my spirit so it could heal my mind and together, we have healed the body as the outcome of the moment.

Most people that know me understand that I come from a place of great humility because I know that the information that is channeled through me is a higher knowing than myself. I have just now begun the journey of ultimate knowing and it has been a long road of doubt, uncertainty, human condition, and, of course, human factor.

Human factor, as it was defined to me, means that we are affected by karma and past life issues that we bring into our life and we let it affect us and our journey. It is the last veil between us and God.

When I first learned about this, I immediately asked that we clear it. "G" put it so well when he said, *"When you stay in the moment on your path and stay present in the light of God, you are free of human factor."* I now understand that the road is about the presence of God within us and about us being present in our life. That means walking in accountability and with intention.

We continually walk oblivious to the real life we desire because we are lost in the repeating patterns of doubt and fear. These patterns are what we must overcome and change. When we are outside the now, the moment, we will repeat patterns of the mundane. It is time to get back to our birthright, to our own place of knowing.

This part has been one of my greatest hurdles to overcome because I did not truly believe that I could be present in my life and affect it so much. In truth, I wanted to stay in the dark and blame the world for my unhappiness. If I truly took accountability for my own life, I would have to start creating. That meant being in the now of my life. The moment of truth is to face up to our choices and when aware, change the situation to the life that we desire.

I realized that I wanted it all - happiness, joy, success, freedom to be me, to have financial independence, and a personal relationship with God. That is my birthright.

This place in the now is the place where creation is. It can only happen in the moment. I've learned that the past is unaffected by the now. But the now is stopped by the past because we tend to live there. The moment that we do that, we are lost to our demons from long ago.

I thought I stood present in my life, but began to realize that what I was doing was holding on to memories because it was the one guarantee that I had. I already knew the outcome. I didn't have to be afraid because I already knew the answer.

When somebody tells me that I have to let go of the familiar and take a chance on myself, that's when I get afraid. Taking a chance on me meant that I would have failed myself if something didn't go quite right. It also meant that I couldn't blame anybody else.

What I forgot is that I needed to forge ahead, to see the uncut road as my contribution to my life, to see that there is not one person who walks exactly like me, not one person who speaks the way I speak. I have an opportunity to create, so the guarantee is me. I guess I have to look at every step I take as unknown, but these steps really become the fruit from the trees that I planted as seeds in my life.

I found myself looking out the window while I was writing this book. One of the things I found interesting was the trees. It is fall here and amazingly enough, I almost missed it because I was so busy rushing, so busy hitting deadlines. If I had waited one more day, I would have missed the most incredible changing of the leaves I have ever seen.

I think what I have realized about being very present in my life is that when I am present, I don't fear. I can be in that place of solving the issue instead of worrying about what tomorrow brings or dredging up the past. I have learned that there is a richness of experience that comes from the knowledge inside of us. If we stay present, we can take from that knowledge and use it to help us make better choices.

I have begun to embrace the wealth of wisdom I have gained from my experiences. I use the past as a place of history, and I use the future as the infinite possibilities that can be. But the only place that I can truly create is in the now, in the moment.

I find it interesting that we know the road walked when we are present in it, but most of the time we are so busy rushing to beat a deadline or rushing to get somewhere that when somebody asks, "Did you see that?" You say, "No, what?"

Somebody asked how we get present in our life. What I told her is we have to slow down long enough to be present, to be its witness, so to speak.

Another question that I once asked "G" was, "Are we continually mirroring to the world, or is the world mirroring to us?" He said, *"Most of the time we don't look in the mirror, we look past it."* He said, *"If you really sat down and looked at yourself in the mirror, you would be in criticism or judgment before you could see who is really looking back at you."*

I tried that and He is right. The first thing I did was find a blemish or a wrinkle. I really didn't want to look into my eyes for I was afraid of what I might see there. So what He had me do is look into the mirror with those same unconditionally loving eyes that He has, and for the first time I didn't hate what I saw.

It is interesting how most of the time we are so busy that we really don't even know each other or the real self. Think about the people that are in our life. Do we really take time to know them or do we just sit and occupy each other's space?

"G" told me once that *"if you captured one moment and then a second moment and placed them side by side, they would become the whole sum of your life."* I wasn't really sure what moments those were. I was too busy being outside of the moment, holding on to the guarantee, the familiar past, or worrying about what tomorrow would bring me. So I decided to take accountability and make every moment count.

I had literally stayed lost because I was so afraid of being alone. I stayed in relationships that I knew were not good for me. I knew it wasn't good for the person I was with, but we stayed because it was familiar. The moment I realized that my happiness or unhappiness was not because of them, but because of me, I had no other choice but to change. I had to quit blaming. I got my life back the moment I walked into it.

The simplest things in life begin when one stops thinking and starts doing. It's funny how the word "present", just in itself, has such a huge impact. It's like present and accounted for. I realize that I'm not always present and I'm not always accounted for. What creates that? I think the reason is because most of the time, I don't take tangible steps to create the desired life.

We must ask our self the questions, "What do we desire in life? What would be our amazing life, our perfect life? Would it be a love affair? Would it be fame and success? Or would it just be quiet contemplation?" Whatever it is, whatever inspires us, whatever ignites the imagination in us, has to start with the single statement, "I am present. I count. My life matters." Those are the simple statements that create the momentum.

What I had heard a very long time ago from a very wise woman was, "Be here. Be a part of it all because if you don't claim your place in the world, there will be no one there to fill that spot."

My mother once said, "In order to change the world, I had to be the light. And with that light, I can light others as we go forward in the journey together." I used to feel that was very ambiguous and really huge. Who would want the responsibility of that?

I did. Look at me, Mom. Here I sit, writing a book about spirituality and new thought which really isn't new. It's just defined differently. Everything leads to the same point. Every road has a destination. Every journey has an outcome. We just have to find our journey, our outcome and be alive in it.

My mom used to say dreams were things we had to hold in the moment because otherwise they would never be realized. I thought about that for a long while. Someone asked "G" once, "How do you hold on to a dream if you are always present?" And "G" answered, *"Creation is held in the moment and what we desire is the manifestation of that dream."*

My life used to be like a huge ocean. When I dove into my life, the ocean, I was fighting to keep my face just above the surface. What I forgot to do was let go of my life as I perceived it. As a result, it kept weighing me down. What I was supposed to do was to discover the true essence of my divine life. The only way that can happen is to be the very intention of my road.

It wasn't until I learned to cast out fear, ask for what I desire, and claim it as mine that I truly saw the face of God. When I stayed in that perpetual state of fear, I felt the absence of God in me and in my life. But the moment that I turned around, I realized he wasn't absent. He was very present, holding me. I was just too caught up in my suffering to be aware of it.

Most of the time humans have to fall so deep into that place of suffering, that place of misery before they can finally decide to get the hell out of it. Why is that? Well, I learned from "G" that the reason we do that is because we are creatures of habit. We don't really like change. Oooh, just the word "change" is scary.

As I said in earlier parts of the book, I ended a very long term relationship and what I found interesting was that everyone in my family was so afraid of me leaving my 26 year marriage that they stopped speaking to me. Somehow, in their eyes, I had done something that was unforgivable.

Now, I don't need to know what that is, but what I have learned is that when someone changes, it forces everyone else to have to look at themselves. Then they do funny things. They might stop speaking to us because they are not ready to look at their life and maybe have to truly admit that there is something wrong in it. Or they may embrace that change like my youngest son did and rise up to meet their own life.

I am not saying that what I did was right or wrong. It was just a catalyst, so to speak. It's what we do with those opportunities in the moment of change, whether we embrace them or deny them, that determine whether we move forward.

I love my family dearly and I have cried many nights, yet could I go back to what was familiar? I don't think so because what I have learned is that sometimes going back means giving up. I have come very far in my journey of self realization to give that up for the old familiar way of life.

My present state of being is to recognize who I am, why I'm here, and that I am the very picture of God walking the journey. We all hear that we have to stay present. We have to be in the now. Now is where it's at. It was through this journey that I began to know it was I who was to learn, and that the journey of enlightenment is not apparent to us, it only begins when we are ready.

Part of what happens to us is that we are all trying to get there, but we are all at different speeds, different stages of readiness. We are all at different levels of awareness, so the journey won't be the same for everyone.

Each person comes to their journey in their own momentum. What we forget is that when we get lost in the past or in the future, it begins to consume us. If we are not careful, we lose the very essence of who we are. So, it's through our birthright, born of all things, that we are loved unconditionally. We have co-creation as part of our very DNA. We are absolute absolution and the very energy of this journey is really our co-creation piece of God. And if the only place that we look at is right now, then what we have to remember is that it is the focused intention of the journey.

When we get complacent, get stuck, we have to stop and not beat ourselves up for being there, but embrace the opportunity and love it. The learning that comes from it is huge because what we have learned so many times is, "been there, done that, not going to do it again."

I have discovered that if I never were to experience life and its moments of difficulty, I would never truly see the tremendous beauty that is around me. The difficulties may not be large or overwhelming. It only takes the tiniest particle of sand, just one, to find its way into the oyster. It begins as a difficulty or an irritant, but the oyster soon embraces the sand. Together they create a beautiful pearl which, in other words, is the gift of our life. That's how we must see our life - embraced and encased, so when we reflect back, we can use it as a tool to help us in the journey instead of a sharp reminder of how painful our past has been.

When I was sixteen years old and I began the journey of finding God, I was on a mission to prove that either He existed or He didn't. It was funny because it was right about that time that I was starting down the road of drugs and doing some pretty stupid things in my life. So the proof that God existed would have to be that He would come and save me or He wouldn't. If He didn't, I would be dead anyway, so it wouldn't really matter.

It was a very pessimistic time in my life. What I learned from drug addiction and alcohol, once I was in recovery, was that we learn how to be very present and live our life one second, one moment, at a time. That is the only way a person can stay sober because if we project forward or back, we tend to fall either into old patterns or new fears. It's what makes us drink or if we're sober, fall off the wagon into drinking again. And that's really not where we want to be.

I know that my sobriety is based on being completely present. Do we forget to see what's in our life, or do we choose not to see it? I think that sometimes we have to look at the vitality of the journey because it's not bogged down by the old. It's like the journey continually changes and grows right before our eyes.

My life transformed the moment I embraced the whole of my life and not just part of it. I stopped settling and started claiming the life that was my birthright. Yes, there have been a lot of changes, and yes, there will continue to be changes, but what I am realizing is that when I embrace those changes, they are actually quite fun. They make me look forward to tomorrow because I'm not holding on to the 'what if's'. I'm holding on to the 'what I haves' and that's what makes the difference.

"G" is right. The very second I held one moment and then captured the next moment, I looked forward to placing them side by side because I knew it was my life. It has made a difference in my life because now I truly understand the wisdom I have gained from living my life to its potential.

Channeling by "G"
"Now"

Note: The following text is transcribed from an actual channeling by "G". The content and grammar is written as spoken by "G".

"G": Hello, this is G. Today's segment is on the momentum of now. Now is that place where all creation exists, where the awakening of your true life begins. So, let us move through to understand the true momentum of a God realized life.

"G": Hello, everyone.
All: Hello, "G".
"G": How are all of you?
All: Very well.

"G": Tonight we are going to talk about the momentum, the power of this world and your ability to create in the now. What does that mean? It means a life fully engaged, a life full of creation, and a life moving forward, each step, one by one, creating each amazing part of your journey. The momentum, which I call now, is really about being in that place of the present. Think about your life. You think about the past a lot, do you not? That's a favorite place for people to be. You worry about what has happened or what you did wrong or then you worry about tomorrow because you may have done something wrong and all of a sudden you worry about what tomorrow will bring. The truth of the journey is that the past is done and the future is God's playground. That's God's world, you have no power in it. The only power you have, the true power, is being placed in the now, in this very moment, as you walk in your life. If you take your hands and put them from your heart straight out, everything between your heart and your hands is yours. Anything beyond your reach, that is God's place. That is where God creates. That is the world that I call God's playground. See, your playground is in your reach. That is your life.

Q: "G", since we struggle to stay present in the moment, what are some benchmarks, some key things that we can hold on to that help us to stay present in our daily life, in our moment?

"G": Very good. Well, think about your thoughts. Your mind tends to be the thing that wanders, the thing that tends to take you places, like the past or the future. One of the greatest gifts that you can have is just to stay where you are. When you are driving your car, your mind tends to wander. Sometimes that is not safe because you're not present when you are driving. And sometimes, do you ever get into your car and you are not really all there and you miss your turn? Well, that's what that is like. When you are in your mind too much, letting your mind talk to you, sometimes you miss the most incredible parts of your life.

So, number one, you must stay present in thought, meaning be aware of your surroundings and what you are looking at, look out the window and the road you are driving down, look at the scenery, be aware of where you are, listen to the music that plays on the radio or maybe on a CD. Sing out loud, that is being present. Those are key things to keeping you present. Sometimes when you think about your day, it takes you out of the moment. Is it interesting that the moment you think about your journey, the habit is to go back to a familiar memory of your life. It is your story that you know well, and it will draw you back to the past.

I always say that when you are first, present and realizing that you are looking out at your life, the second thing that you must remember in this, is that when you are not present, and you catch yourself thinking or wandering, don't beat yourself up for it. That is not a good thing. What you need to do is recognize that your mind wandered, call it back, put yourself in the moment right here, right now. Think about the flower that you are looking at or a conversation that you are having with somebody. When you are talking to them, truly be engaged in the conversation. Be present in it; listen to every word. Don't be in your head formulating an opinion or thinking about what you are going to say next. If you are really present and truly listening, instead of just hearing, you will really be a part of the moment, the now.

The third thing that I always recommend people to do is that when you find yourself getting into a place where you feel judgment or fear or whatever, those places that take you out of the moment, ask yourself this key question, "Can I change it? My thoughts running over it and over it and over it again, like a wheel, does that change the event?" No. What changes the event is not running back and forth in your head, but maybe doing tangible steps: walking, saying, "This is what I am going to do to get myself wherever I need to be" because truly being present means being in the road and walking it, not sitting and going, "Oh, my life sucks." "Oh, this is bad." "Oh, I don't know where money is going to come from; what am I going to do?" "Oh, my God, the client didn't call. Oh, no, no." When you do that, what is that? It's taking you completely out of solving it and putting you into chaos. It takes you out of the control.

So, the key to it is to stay in control of your car, your vessel, you, your life. It is to first and foremost recognize that you cannot change it by sitting there mulling it over in your head. The true control is taking the steps to change something. If you realize that you are worried about money, do the legwork that will help you get out of the worry, whether it is looking in your bank account, calling people, talking to someone, getting yourself very present in it.

Then, number four, turn it over to God. God will take care of you if you do the legwork. Legwork is all those tangible things you can do to create. For example, if you desire a new job, legwork could include making a list of what the perfect job is for you, updating a resume, sending it out to potential employers, looking at want ads or working with a head hunter, putting the word out that you're looking for a new job, asking for the perfect job during meditation for your highest good and with great ease, etc.

Perhaps you have a fear around something, say money, which is always a big thing for people because they're worried about paying their bills. And let's say you're not sure what you're going to do. You have five dollars in your bank account and you need fifty to pay a bill because you've got creditors beating on your door. Well, instead of getting into the fear that creditors is beating at your door, realize that you can't do anything about it. They're there and that's OK. But what you can do is not put the energy into fearing them getting to you, coming to you, doing something to you. What you have to do is call, figure out a way of making the issue different like let's say you have a skill. Now everyone here has a skill, correct? And if you are sitting there looking at an empty bank account and there are bills on the table that need to be paid, the best way to solve the issue is by figuring out what you can do to make it better. Maybe you do massage, or maybe you borrowed money to somebody a while back. Make phone calls. Talk to people. Do these things. Do the legwork. And when you're all done and you've done all the legwork, put all your feelers out there, get quiet, and ask God for highest good and with great ease because He knows things that you don't.

There is an answer, as long as you are doing the legwork in your space of solving the problem. When you are done, meditate on that and say, "OK, God, I did the legwork. I made all the calls. I did everything that I was supposed to do. Now I am going to turn this over to you and I am going to let it go." And the moment that you let it go, you give it to God's playground because it was beyond your reach, wasn't it? You could only do just the legwork in the space that you could solve the issue. Now, it's time to let it go and give it to "G" or to God.

What do I mean by give it to God? Think about when you are sitting in your life and you are trying to come up with an answer to something and you say, "I don't know. There is no use in this. I don't even know what the heck...." What is that doing? That is giving up. But that's not giving up in a way that is positive. It's giving up with hopelessness. When you say "I have done all that I can and I have faith," faith takes it to the next level of turning it over and knowing that God will provide. It's saying that you have faith in yourself that you have done your part and now you are allowing God to do His part or Its part and when that happens, the doors to the universe open up and you will be amazed at what falls into your lap. Lots of times, what you don't even realize, is that you have limited resources. You only know up to your level of awareness, but because God is all knowing and has the whole of the universe to tap into for resources, you might be amazed at where the money will come from or how this problem might be solved that you never expected. You will say "I never thought this could be this way."

Q: "G", I'm thinking about what you said about faith and God's playground and being in the moment and I am wondering if you can put this a little bit more together for me. What I am contemplating now is that maybe what happens in my life is that as things come up in my day, if I'm not present enough and have enough faith that it is taken care of, then I'm not letting it go so it can't go into God's playground and it resides within my space, kind of in limbo?

"G": Yes. We call that suspended. Unresolved issues suspend around you until finally the issue is forced to be resolved. Think about it like this. When you are having a problem and you keep mulling it over and mulling it over and you say "I let it go, I let it go", the fact that you keep mulling it over and saying 'I let it go' proves you haven't let it go. Or, you've let it go, but keep taking it back.

Now I will tell you a little story to kind of help pull it all together. The story goes like this. A little boy has a toy and this toy is like a pull toy. Do you remember when children used to have a string and they would pull the toy and it would be like a bear and as the bear went a little drum would go dinka, dinka, dinka? Well, one day this little boy was pulling his bear along and the bear started going dink…dink…dink instead of dinka, dinka, dinka. So, what happened was, he went to his grandfather and said "Grandfather, my toy is broken. I need you to fix it." And the grandfather says, "Then give it to me. I will fix it." And the little boy gave the toy to his grandfather but, you know that string? He held onto it and he held on and held on and when finally he got so tired of waiting for Grandfather to fix it, he yanked it back from him and looked at his grandfather and said "Grandfather, I gave you this toy, but you never fixed it." And he says, "Child, how can I fix it when you would never let go?" That is as simple as it is and as very complex as it can be. You have to look at life like that. When you give something to God, give it. Don't give it and hang on and give it and hang on because you never really truly let go with faith. You continually hold on with skepticism, doubt, fear.

Q: "G", so if I'm unaware that I'm doing this, how do I realize or get in touch with the fact that I'm hanging on or have something suspended?

"G": Think about things that you think about in your day when your mind wanders. Think about driving down the road and you see a car accident and go "Ooooh, that's bad." And you have a little fear that it could happen to you. Even though you didn't really put much thought into it before you let it go, you thought about it and you gave it emotion, because you had fear. Well, what happens to that is it might be hanging out there around you, floating along until the situation is perfect like when you have some fear going on, there is a chaos in your life, you've got some unresolved issues happening, your life is kind of in a little bit of turmoil or I always like this one, when people say, "You know, it's always funny, when something bad happens..." What do you say?

Q: It happens in threes.

"G": Yes, or they say "You know when shit hits the fan, it really hits the fan." I always hear people say this and I always say "Oh, be so careful." So you think about those things that you've said all through your life or heard other people say. So, all of a sudden you're driving down the road and someone comes along and you tap on your brakes and they don't see it and wham-o, they hit you from behind and the very accident you fear becomes a real outcome. That is what we call suspended. Things don't always happen right away. Conditions have to be perfect, you know. That is always the rule of creation. The circumstances and all the elements around it have to be perfect before it is created, good or bad, because you see, the moment, the now, is the outcome of your life. The present, the very present of your life, is the moment of your creation and the momentum of your outcome and it all resides together. So when things are going along in life, guaranteed, the outcome is there right in front of you.

Q: "G", if I am looking for a job and I'm working at it and I'm doing everything that I can do in my space and then I turn it over and sit back in doubt that I didn't do enough or that I should be doing this or I should be doing that, how do I quit the cycle of believing that I need to keep doing something?

"G": Very good. Here's what happens. Man does what we call overkill. This is what you do. When you have something going on in your life and you have to get something done, we sit there and watch you and you do overkill. Simple is as simple does. I have said that before. It is said all the time. It has been said in movies even. You see, the simpler the things you do, the quicker things happen for you. But see, mankind likes to do things in triplicate. Mankind likes to do things in multiples of ten.

God gives you one law and that one law, given to you by God, gives you prosperity as well as lack. The same thing goes with health; the same law that gives you good health is the same law that gives you sickness. But man goes out and says, "Well, it couldn't be just one law, we need ten." Man goes, "Of course, that's not enough" so you create Ten Commandments and you've got to really fill it in. Then of course the Ten Commandments aren't good enough so you have to have those seven deadly sins too. You've got to add on to them so you can really feel bad. I love that one.

But the reality of the journey is that it is very simple. When you have a mission, something that you want done, like find a new job, and you've done your resume, and you've sent it out, and you've put it on some website, or maybe you go and have an interview with somebody, and you turn it over and have said, "I have done all that I can," say "Now I have a leap of faith".

When you catch yourself going back to that place of "Oh, I haven't heard from them. Maybe I didn't do enough," you have to stop and recognize that you are back in the cycle of repeating the pattern of needing to do more.

Second, once you recognize that you're in that pattern again, you have to do something that is going to get you back out of it. Like I always say, it's a good thing we have reverse because sometimes you need to back up a little bit because you're in something that you shouldn't be in, like God's playground, and that's too far. So, now you have to back up and be present in your life. The future, that's God's playground. You need to back up because that's not your space. But what is your space is the moment, is the now. Now! And so, when you catch yourself doing this repeating pattern of "I didn't do enough" or "I get into fear" I always say, have a conversation with God. Say "God, I am talking to you because I can feel myself spinning into fear and I need assistance in bringing me back to that place where I no longer am walking in fear and walking in all that chaos of 'what if'". Get quiet and listen. Go into your heart. When you get quiet and go into the heart, it is amazing how the mind quiets, how the heartbeat slows, and the fast pace of fear goes away, and you become present in the very unconditional love that is your birthright.

These steps, folks, are being accountable. See, most people are not accountable about their life, they feel responsible which is not their domain. It is not your place. Accountability is in the now, responsibility, think about that, is out here. It is out of your reach. Sensibility is guilt. Sensibility is the past.

Q: "G", could you explain the difference between accountability and responsibility?

"G": Yes. This is a good one because what happens is, you feel responsible for the world; you feel responsible for your family members; you feel responsible for everything that is in front of you, your job, everything. But the reality of it is, the only thing that you are truly accountable for is you. Yes, you have to take care of your family and your children but that's not your responsibility. Accountability means being present in your space, staying present in the now. Responsibility is caused by a series of sensibilities. You know how you learn from your family of origin that "children should be seen and not heard?" Or you hear the statement that says "men should be the breadwinner and the women should stay and take care of home and house"?

Well, if you think about those things and those are the things that you base the foundation of your knowing on, what happens to you? Your sensibility says when you're not doing that, you feel guilt. When you are not doing what the Bible or this book or that talk show host, or this thing over here, or that thing over there, or a friend, says, when you're not doing what they feel is right, you get into responsibility and all of a sudden, the next thing you know, you're out there trying to fix the world. "Well, you know, I really am responsible for fixing the world because I screwed it up." That's what happens to you. You get into this place of guilt or obligation. The only obligation you have is to work on changing you. The only thing is, it's not responsibility, but accountability. It's staying in your heart and saying "I'm accountable to me." To truly make a difference in the world is to stand in that place of accountability, holding to what you know is your own truth, and being the light.

Q: "G", I need a little bit of clarity. So, are you saying that when I am in a place of accountability, if I have children, I am going to be doing things that honor me such as feeding them and paying the bills because I am accountable for myself and instead of having emotion around it, I see it as part of who I am? But when I look at is as responsibility, like I've got to make them food, then there is emotion behind it that is fed by obligation?

"G": Yes. Think of it like this. When you are in your life and you put your life as a priority, everything falls into place and fits like a puzzle, but when you are in responsibility, you are trying to figure out how to get that in there, get this done, get that done. The next thing you know, the puzzle pieces don't fit because you are doing "G"'s job or God's job. See, the responsibility of the whole is that as long as you put your life as a priority, and you say "This is my life, this is who I am" and everything is all encompassed into that, God opens the door like a wind that blows every puzzle piece into place, and no longer is it a conflict, no longer do you have to fight to fit it in. Part of all of this is, when you are in a negative state, that is fighting the conflict and that is fighting the "G" or the God that helps you. Think about the God within, the "G" within. That is what you need to make important, number one, first. And what you teach the people around you is how to hold to that very same light, to hold themselves accountable to their own life, and then they open the door and say "I am God inside. I have an indwelling God inside and I am, right now, my life."

Q: "G", I hear you say "the God within" and I can hear that with my mind. How do I go from my mind to my heart to know that God is within?

"G": Very good. How it works is that when you are in your head, obviously you know that is not God. That is as we have all talked about, that unique soul energy, that unique you, that personality that is running around doing what it needs to do. But to find the indwelling God, to find the presence of God within, ahh. Think about what your mind does. You go out in the world and are going along and all of a sudden somebody asks you to do something. The first thing you should do is go into your heart. You do and hear that first answer that says "Don't do it", but you don't listen to that very first feeling. What you do is you let that mind go, "Well, you know. If you go and do this, maybe you might have some fun." Do you know what I'm talking about? Well, all of a sudden you go. And it was a bust, it was so bad. You knew you shouldn't have gone, but you didn't listen; you went anyway. Of course, the lesson was what? To learn that you needed to listen to that very first feeling, that heart knowing that said "Don't go." That is your indwelling God, your divine spirit, telling you, letting you know, in that very moment, what the right answer is.

You say, "No, it's not that simple. You don't understand, G." That's what I hear people say. "It couldn't be that simple, "G"." "You know I want to believe this, I want to believe that it is that simple." Well, it is, because part of what you have to recognize is that when you are not present in your life and honoring your spirit, how does your life feel? Crappy, out of control. You don't feel like you have any say in it. When you are present in the indwelling God, this place of now, this place of you, this accountability, this life right out in front of you, all of a sudden the mind quiets, the heart truly expresses and that is the indwelling God. That is the part that steps forward.

You see, many students who have come to me have been working on bringing in the master higher self and people say "Oh, what's that, "G"?" Well, what that is, is the divine spirit, the all knowing spirit of you. That is that piece of God, brought down in you. But see, you get busy in life, you get rushing here and rushing there, and going here and doing that and you forget this place here inside of you. You forget how this really is truly spirit's will and like I said in previous channelings, spirit's will is the true knowing of God. It is that part of God within and when you govern that and when you make choices based on a quiet mind and not on emotion, but on the heart, that is when you will make the right choice to walk the road in the right way.

Q: So, "G", are you telling me that the heart and emotion are two separate things?

"G": Yes, the two are different. The heart is that place of complete acceptance, unconditional love, no judgment, no critical thought. It just loves you, loves you. And emotion, it is a tool. But see, you run rampant with the tool and think that's what it is and it's not. Don't run rampant with a tool. Has your mother said, "Don't run with the scissors. It's sharp. Don't run with a knife." But that's kind of what you do. Emotion, when it runs wild, creates all kinds of chaos.

See, you know how I said in the earlier channelings that there are words, thoughts, feelings, emotions? Well, one of the things I always explain about creation concerns words and thoughts. You speak them, you think about them. And here's God going "Man, I heard that word, lack. Oh, I heard sick." And those words roll around in your head and you're starting to think about them. Well, the truth of it is when that lets go and drops down into the heart, which I call the feeling center, which is the true God knowing, the true indwelling God, it has to take note, it has to take notice. And what happens is, when it recognizes that there is something to this, all of a sudden it says "Hmmm, I need to listen." And then you get emotion involved and emotion is the kick start, the push that pushes it out into your life so God acts upon it.

So think about this. You have two choices when you create. You have one hanging on the left, and one hanging on the right. OK? Here they are. On the left side, that is mind's choice and on the right side might be spirit's will. Here they hang and all of a sudden you're in that place where you have to decide which side it will be. Most of the time, guess what people do? They choose mind's choice. It is the first place they go. They pick this one because mind's choice is the chaos; mind's choice is fear; mind's choice is lack and all those similar things you are familiar with. And by choosing that, that is what you create. But if you truly allow the spirit's will to take hold, it will then bring forward all that you desire. The spirit's will is what your divine spirit knows is for your highest good and with great ease. Spirit's will communicates with you through the heart.

Q: So, "G", I've been listening to what you've said about accountability and responsibility. I grew up in a family where I was taught my responsibility was to provide for my family.

"G": Think about your life and when you are in your life, creating a series of things. You were just asking the question about responsibility, that your life had taught you that you were responsible for taking care of family and taking care of them as your job. Well, this then takes it to a place of a negative because when you feel an obligation, it doesn't come from the heart, it comes from that place of the mind.

And when you think about all the things you have been taught, all the things that you have been told you must do, it almost feels a little resentful that you have to do it. Then you are in the momentum of having to do something because you think it's your job and you think this because you hear the statement that it's the man's responsibility to be the breadwinner and to take care of the household and it's a woman's responsibility to take care of child and home. It's not like that. What it is about is very much being in that place inside of you, that accountability that says "I am living my life, not out of a sense of duty or responsibility, but out of a place of knowing in my heart that I am happy, that I am in joy, that I am creating this life and I love my life and my life loves me back."

The only thing that you are accountable for in your life is you. You see, the family part comes automatic. Your life becomes the things you love. You become in love with life and it's no longer a job, it's no longer a responsibility. It is that place that says 'I am the life I live."

Q: So, what I am hearing for myself is that being accountable means that I am choosing moment by moment to take all of my life as one piece and choosing to make it my life?

"G": Absolutely. Absolutely. See, life has to be something that you love to be in, not a burden, not a heavy weight that weighs you down. See, one of the greatest things I can teach mankind, if they are open to hearing the truth of their life, is that all the things that they have learned can be erased. All the things that they have built their life upon can be changed. I know that you can't unknow what you know. I have said that before and I will say that again, but what you can do is rephrase it, change it, take the old way and move it to a new understanding of a life you desire to live. That's what it's about.

Q: So we have the ability to transform our lives and everything we have ever been taught into something better, higher?

"G": Yes. Think about how you want your life. How many people in this place in this world desire to have the kind of life that nourishes them, gives them a sense of being, a sense of knowing inside themselves. Most people are looking to find themselves, to find God, to find who they are. Well, I will tell you this. God resides in the now. God resides in the present. It is not out in the future and it is not in the past. Sure there is reference to the past and sure there is the great unknown of the future, but God does not reside in either place. God is in the moment. I have said this before, but this is a new concept to a lot of people. Time does not exist in the realm of spirit, so, if God is spirit, everything co-exists in the moment. So, the moment, the now, is really the place of God's creation.

Q: What if I want something in the future? I can't have it since I must stay in the now?

"G": Understand there is a difference between the words want, need and desire. To want places it out of you, out of reach because it implies you don't have. It is lack. A need is more desperate than a want, but it too comes from a place of lack. Desire comes from that place of hope inside. It is not desperate, nor does it imply you don't have it because you don't have the money. It changes the momentum and creates, in the now, everything you desire.

Q: "G", if I have the accountability of paying for my rent, paying for utilities, paying for my car payments, paying for my insurance and I am in an occupation that I'm not happy with, how should I be thinking in the moment to create the ability to find what my passion and desire is, and move over to that occupation fast enough in order to sustain my overhead, so to speak?

"G": Very good. This one is probably the key to what it truly is all about. You see, the first thing that people make the mistake in is not giving thanks for what they have. See, when you are in a job that you just hate, it's really hard to move out of it. So, what you have to do is find what you love about it because the more that you dislike it, the more likely it is you dig in with spurs and don't leave it. So, part of it is, the biggest change, is to find the things that you love about the job so that you can let it go.

Most of the time, you are so good at holding on to the negative that you stay there for a long time. Like, you're in a relationship and you're in it for who knows how long, fifteen, twenty, thirty years and you're in that relationship because it's familiar. It is something that you know. It is something that is easy to do. You know the routine: you get up, go, do, all the time. And when the unknown comes to you, like let's say you want to change careers or let's say you're not happy and you decide to become happy, that fear out there can loom for a while. But what you have to start to do is not hold to the fear of the unknown. Recognize that every day you wake up is an unknown of what your day is going to be.

When you stay present in the now, in the moment, there is nothing to fear because you are always present where you need to be and your foot goes wherever you tell it to go and your life goes wherever you direct it to be. Yes, there are overheads and costs that you have to take care of.

That is part of life, all these things that you have to take care of.

This is the best way to take care of it. Make a list of all the things you love to do. Think about what you're good at. I bet everybody in this room or on the planet has a list a mile long of all the things they love to do, but they don't even know they have the skills to do it. It's recognizing the skills you have and what you love to do. With a knowing you're doing the legwork, still honor the job you have. See, most people, I tell them to take a leap of faith, but they are not ready to take a leap of faith, so you've got to take baby steps. You know, little tiny baby steps. The little tiny baby step is go part time, maybe do it on a Saturday or maybe on a week night. You take them small because when you're not ready to take a leap of faith, you will get scared and you will fail at it. So the key to really moving into something you love is small baby steps.

How many people here have a favorite food? Ok, everybody in the room has their favorite food? Like that 'chunky monkey' ice cream they have at the store and you go and have one bite and say "I'm only going to have one bite" and you take one bite and say "Oh, this is too good" then you have another bite and another bite and then you end up eating the whole thing? Well, think of it like that. See 'chunky monkey' is a pretty extreme example, but when you do something you love or something that you really enjoy, it no longer is forcing you to choke down brussels sprouts. It means really loving what you do and that doesn't feel like a job.

I will tell you a story about a young woman who had come to "G" a long time ago and she was working in corporate America. Now it was a big company that she worked for. She kept saying "You know, I really desire to do the "G" work. I really desire to do this. I really desire to do that." And she kept saying "I desire it "G", I desire it."

She kept saying this whenever she got quiet. She held it in her heart. And then one day, she was sitting there in a job that she was really not happy with and the Universe kept hearing her say "You know, I'm really not happy here. OK, there are things I love about the job. I love the people, I love this." There were things that she loved so she had found those things she loved and the Universe heard that. And the Universe said "OK, she is finding what she loves about it. Now it's time to get her to move." And she kept saying, "I've got to do this."

It's kind of funny how the Universe can make things happen that make you have to move on when you're not letting go. All of a sudden, just out of sheer determination, Source brings a boss that could be probably what you would call the boss from hell. She realized this because she was a good director and she did her job well. She had taken the company in the beginning from being very small to very big and then bought by an even bigger company. Out of her amazing abilities as an operations director, she was honored by getting a bonus of over $200,000 at the time of the sale by the people who sold the business. They told her "We would not be here if it had not been for you."

See at that time she was happy, but when things changed in her life she would say, "Oh, I just have to find something different. I desire to do something I really love." So, she was sitting there and the new boss was saying things that were very hurtful. She knew they weren't real. She knew they weren't true. She remembered the whole six years that she was with the company, how she had gotten praised and bonuses and awards for all the amazing work she had done. So, she knew that this chief operating officer, this person who was her new boss, really was not for her highest good.

One day she thought about what she wanted and how she was being treated and said "I really need to have a leap of faith." Now I don't tell people to take a leap of faith unless they really have a leap of faith, but she really had a leap of faith and she leapt herself right out of the job. She went in, gave notice, did all her parts, and left, and believe it or not, she is now in the momentum of her own life, creating the life she loves and the life she lives so it is all good. Her life transformed because she had enough faith that when she took the leap, God, Source, Light would provide for her. And because of that faith, God, Source, Light provided her with more money in many different ways during the first six months after she left than she had made in an entire year at her six figure job in corporate America. See, Source is creative. But she held to it. She knew, without a doubt, that she would be cared for. When you have that much faith in something, that's the time to take a leap.

If you don't have that kind of faith, but you have, what I call, bursts of faith…that's usually what most people have is bursts of faith…that's when you create in little steps, like working part time, while building your new business, building the new life for yourself. And when you have those little bursts of faith, that's when you leap and do something new. And then you go and still have your job and eventually, once you're ready, the Universe can kind of know something that you don't. It knows when your heart is really ready to take the leap and all of a sudden the answer comes. Now if you say with highest good and great ease, you won't have the boss from hell to push you out of a job. It might have been just as simple as deciding "You know what? I'm done here and I'm leaving." But sometimes people forget to say for highest good and great ease so it's very important that you say that whenever you are asking for change or new momentum or going into that leap of faith for highest good and with great ease. It will always be that nice soft spot of God that will help catch you when you fall down.

So, that would be my best way of explaining how you can transition from still being accountable for your life, but yet now you get a taste. As that small business builds you will be able to pull back hours or sometimes you will be full time and go part time, and then you will all of a sudden go no time because now you are in the life that you love and the life that loves you.

Q: So, what you are saying "G", even though things seem to be going wrong, there is always a gift behind it to come out in the future and blossom?

"G": Yes. See, you have to see all good in all bad because they really are the gifts of your life. You know what I always say. If you can embrace the things that you may not see as such a good thing at the time, if you find the gift in it, see what is positive about it, you change that momentum and create new positives in your moment, in your now. See, when you hold onto negative, you keep creating negative and so your now, your moment, is all full of crap and you sit there going, "Oh, I don't understand it."
    I will tell you this funny story I heard a long time ago from a woman who was telling the story and said, "I heard this joke once. This man walks up and sees this little boy and this little boy is sitting there digging in a great big pile of manure. The man stood there watching the little boy dig and dig and dig and he finally says, "Son, what are you doing?" And the boy said, "With all this manure, there has to be a horse in here somewhere." So you see, he saw the gift in the manure.

Q: So, "G" is it good to say 'thank you' for the gift even if I don't know exactly what the gift is?

"G": Absolutely. One of the greatest things that can transform or change a negative is by giving thanks or blessing the situation even if you may not see it at the time because sometimes it's not so obvious to you why it happened. Say you are sitting there in the shadows of your life with clouds and rain all around you. It has rained for days. Then all of a sudden the rain stops. It's still cloudy, but something clears the vision a little bit. You look out and see a flower breaking the surface of the soil because the rain finally nurtured the ground. What does this mean? It means that though you saw the rain as something negative, the gift is that the flower does get nourished. So see the positives in those things because they will change you.

    I remember a young woman who said that she was abused and said "I cannot see the gift in being abused. You cannot tell me, "G", that that is good." And I said to her, "You cannot see the good in it because you refuse to forgive. You refuse to let go and you will walk in your life angry, bitter, maybe even a point of sadness or continually in fear because every time you turn a corner you will never find happiness." And she said, "Well, I guess that is what I will have to do." But she kept coming to "G", you know. She didn't stop because there must have been a message, a little seed I planted in her because she came back and was sitting there and still kind of frowning, but she kept coming back. It's interesting what happens to people when they do that because little by little in the room, people who are listening, who are enlightened, who are of like mind, get up and tell their story or get up and speak their heart or listen to something that "G" says that changes something inside of them and all of a sudden, one little word came out and the woman changed. And that one word that transformed her life was acceptance and the understanding of the word acceptance.

"G" had told the group a long time ago that the eyes are an illusion that when you look out into the world, it's not always what you see. Sometimes when you look out into the world, you can't trust your eyes. They might be clouded by your feelings and your emotions. They might be clouded by all the things that you have experienced in life. The veils have dropped over your eyes and you cannot see and all this time her coming and saying she could not see, she could not understand, is exactly what happened.

But I talked about acceptance that night and I explained to her acceptance can only be truly experienced in the place of now because when you are in here, in the moment of your life, the past is all gone, you can't look back. Acceptance cannot fall back. It's done and acceptance cannot see into the future for it's not set. But what you do have is the acceptance of the moment. Embrace the fact that you are sitting here breathing in and out, around people who love you and that you love, that you are finally making steps to change, to transform, to move forward in your life.

In that very moment she understood that the gift of her life was that she was here. Many times she had wanted to end her life, to check out. The gift was she realized she had a choice. She didn't think she did and finally she said "What can I do "G" to really change how I feel?" And I said, "The first thing you need to do is write a letter of forgiveness to yourself. The moment you forgive yourself for all the things that you have done to yourself, is when you can truly forgive others that are out there and in your life. You will begin to see with true acceptance and true understanding because this place right here is the life that you live. If you are carrying the past, the past will always reside in the moment and in the now; and if you continually live in the future and project into the future, you will never be able to be effective now in the moment because you will always be outside of it. You can't be outside your life anymore. You have to be in your life, walking it, conscious, knowing that everything that you do is a conscious intention of the road. The moment, the now, is that place where conscious awareness lives."

Q: We have been talking about the now and one thing that comes to mind is, if I have a really bad cold or someone is in pain or something, you can't help but feel like you're really in the now because you're experiencing it at the time. How do you change that so it doesn't stay there?

"G": So, what you're asking is, how does this apply to health? Well, health is just a symptom of a thought, a word, and maybe even an old pattern like if somebody says "It runs in the family; it's genetic." You know how that is? I had a woman who came to "G" and she had terrible back pain. It was very, very bad and she was just hurting and she kept saying ""G", it's like a knife in my back." She does not take meds. She does not take any aspirin or anything like that. I told her "Why do you not take it?" She said that she should have enough faith to command it gone. I said to her, "How much faith do you have?" And she said, "I don't know." And I said, "You know, God does not sit there and say go without just because you don't have faith." What it is, is like assistance.

When you are in pain, it is very difficult to let go of something, to turn it over to God. So sometimes you need to take an aspirin or ibuprofen or Tylenol. Sometimes you need to do those things to help to alleviate the pain long enough. Most of the time, when you are in the bowels of pain, deep into pain, you can't see the light. You're almost overcome with it.

What you have to do though is allow yourself to be assisted so that you can get out of the cloud of your mind that is telling you "this hurts". Your body is saying, "I know" and your head says, "this hurts" and your body says, "I know" and your spirit is up there going "let it go, let it go." And you're going "I don't hear that, I hear pain. I just feel the pain." So sometimes you need to have assistance. But it you have to, that's not a failure on the part of faith. What it is though, is you are human here and you get caught up in the creation of colds or the creation of back pain because you feel guilt.

You know, upper back pain is representative of guilt. So, when you have guilt obviously all of a sudden your back goes out and you're all of a sudden sitting there dealing with it. When you are in pain, I am not telling you to go cold turkey and go without just because that means you don't have faith. Use assistance, use the doctors and get the help that you need because it's vital to getting you out of the cloud you have created."

Q: Then asking others for a healing would not be a failure of faith either?

"G": No. Because part of all of this is really realizing that you do not have to do this alone. You're not an island unto yourself. You really are a connection of each other, an extension of each other. And so, when you need help or you need assistance, you need to realize that all these things are not to do alone. Do I not say, turn it over to God, hold to the indwelling God, ask for those things that you desire in life? I'm not telling you to go out and suffer just because you do not have that faith. Sometimes you need assistance.

Remember I was saying earlier how when you have a job and you want this perfect job, but you don't have faith enough to leap out of your job and just go with your new job, you have to take little baby steps to things. That's how it is. That is how your life is. Sometimes there are people out there who can take that leap of faith and you go "I want to be able to do that". Well, OK. It takes what we call an act of faith to get there and that act of faith is just like, as you say, 'act as if'. That is an act of faith. This is new because you have heard leap of faith and you always hear "G" say "act as if and it becomes." Well that is an act of faith. An act of faith says, "I am holding to this and I need a little assistance in holding it." That's an act of faith.

Q: So, "G", does all of this apply to chronic diseases too?

"G": That is a very good question. A few years ago, a woman came to "G" and was very excited and had been learning a great deal about her life and her road and accountability. So it had been a road that she had dedicated to her life, to the journey of finding herself, finding the self realized self and finding the God realized journey. A few months ago she had rolled over in bed one night and discovered that she had a lump in her breast. At first she didn't want to go with fear, but there was that little ping. She went "No, no, no." She decided that she needed to get a doctor to look at it.

She immediately went in and went to the doctor and she was told that she had breast cancer. Of course she was very fearful at first, but she decided not to let fear get her. She decided to stay in the moment and walk in fearlessness. What I mean by that is that she cast the fear aside and knew, without any doubt at all, that she would come through this and she would survive this.

Now, you have to understand, to her family of history, her family of origin, that wasn't so good. She had lost a mother to breast cancer, an aunt to breast cancer, and a grandmother to breast cancer. As a result, she had many people, her father included, who were very afraid that she was going to meet that same fate. Well, she came to "G", very upset, and she started to cry and she said ""G", I have walked this road. I have done all that you have asked. Why would this happen to me?" I explained to her that she had, at some point in her life, had a fear that she would be just like her mother and get cancer and all of a sudden, not realizing that this fear about getting cancer was still suspended around her, manifested in her life. Now, she could fall into this place that says, "Oh, my God, I'm going to die of this" or she could choose the road that says, "I will survive. I am fearless. I am walking this road." She chose the latter. She came to "G" and said, ""G", there are two things I want to make sure happen. I want to keep my breasts and I want to keep my hair." And "G" said, "It is done." And so she went to the doctor who told her what her treatment options were.

She chose a lumpectomy without radiation because she believed her faith was strong enough to heal the cancer with just the lumpectomy. After the surgery was a success, she had another session with her oncologist. The doctor said to her "If you do not have this radiation, I would hold fear for you forever because I know some day you will get this back and it will wreak havoc in your whole body and you will die from this."

Now, of course, she came to see "G" after she had this session with her doctor and she said ""G", what do I do? I want to hold fearlessness, but this doctor is holding fear and even my family is holding fear and I don't know if I am strong enough to hold fearlessness that much." And I said to her "Do you truly believe that if you have radiation treatments that it is failure? That it is not being truly successful in the road?" She sat there for a moment and said "Well, yes, I guess I kind of do" and I told her it wasn't failure. Do you remember earlier when I said that sometimes when you are in pain, you need to take an aspirin? Well, this is the same thing. Sometimes you have to do treatments, with your fearlessness, to truly become the success story she is.

Today she is cancer free and she literally got to keep her breasts and her hair and her life. So, you see, she was fearless in the face of something that most people would run from and fall deep into fear with. She is the success story. She stayed present. She stayed in the moment. She didn't run with fear of the past. She did not accept their future. She decided to do the treatment and truly understand that she was fearless and she is an example to the rest of the world that says "I held fearlessness and mine became successful."

That goes with all disease. Disease is really the product of something you have feared, something you have suspended, something you have accepted from family of origin or something you have seen on TV or books you read. If you truly believe that you are going to get cancer because it runs in your family or heart disease that runs in your family or if you believe that arthritis is crippling, what do you think the Universe will bring to you? That which you believe. Like all diseases you hold in yourself, when you are in that place where you are facing a disease or facing an illness, because of a moment of lapse or a moment where you gave in to some fear, don't hold it with guilt. Don't hold it with all these things.

You need to go forward holding faith. You know I said that leap of faith? Well leap of faith is one thing, but you also have to be in that place of knowing that this is an act of faith. When you go to the doctor, you take your pill and you hold that it will do what it is supposed to do. That is an act of faith.

Q: "G", you talk about things that are suspended around us and they show up in our life later on and we don't even know it's suspended. Is there a way to bypass what we have already suspended around us so that it does not show up in our lives?

"G": You have to understand that I have given what they call a release statement to use that a person can say if they are thinking a negative thought or if something happens to them. The release statement is:

> "God, anything that I may have said, spoken ill, thought, felt, emoted or did that is contrary to my highest good, or anything suppressed, repressed, suspended or hanging around that is contrary to my highest good, I release it all to you now for my highest good and with great ease."

Now this statement releases things that might come up or might flare up in your life. What you have to understand is this statement will help you from not doing things that might retrigger an old, past, suspended issue. The only time the past retriggers and comes into your life is if you are holding to a certain fear, a certain age somebody you know went through breast cancer, somebody you know who had a heart attack. You see what I am saying? Now I know the young woman I was talking about who had recently overcome breast cancer, her friend had just had, within a year before, a double mastectomy because of breast cancer. Now the reason it triggered in her was because of that suspended thing a long time ago and it just rekindled a memory in her. That's why I say use the release statement throughout the day so that you do not have to repeat something suspended from before.

Q: OK, "G", so I am getting a flash bulb here. The more present that I become in my life and the more practice that I have in walking my road fully present, the more I mitigate old suspended fears, doubts, non-productives from popping up in my life?

"G": Absolutely. That is why it is so vital to be present and in your life. When you are in the past, what happens to you? You regurgitate the past. If you are fearful of the future and are always in that unknown state, these are things you attract to yourself, the things you fear, the things you doubt. But when you are present, in the now, fear cannot be. It is amazing because when you are present in the very moment of who you are, fear cannot reside there because you are in the action of creating your life. You are in the momentum of one foot in front of the other, being aware of a sunrise, being aware of a sunset, being aware of what differences you make by the words you speak, the things you think, the roads you walk. I always have heard this: "If you do not like the play that is playing before you, you have two choices; one, you get off the stage, or two, change your role in it." Don't continue to be in a play or in an act that does not speak to you. You must walk in the honored life of yourself because being in that honor of you, others and God, when you stay present in that state of being which is being in the conscious heart, being present in your heart, these things cannot come up.

Q: So, then "G", my question is, if you are truly in the momentum of the moment, is there a state of grace that is related to these things we are talking about?

"G": Certainly. What I know to be is that most people do not realize that when you are in the moment, you are in a permanent state of grace. Grace is not like the grace you understand in old biblical times or in religion, but grace is God holding you up, lifting you out of and raising you above the mundane of your life, raising you up out of the non-productive things that pull you back. God raises you up out of the undertow of a wave so that you can ride the top of the wave until you reach the shore.

Q: So, "G", you talk about being in the moment and how being in that state of grace is so important. What if I fall out of that? Do I have to be in that all the time to be able to create? Can you help me with that?

"G": A state of grace is really the outcome of being present, of being in you and being very much a part of your life. You can create. You don't have to be in grace to create because your whole life is a creation, honestly. You think a negative thought, you're not in grace, but you're out there creating. That same law that brings you wealth, brings you lack or brings you poverty. So, you have to understand that God loves unconditionally. He does not discriminate. He sees you all as equal and all as the same and if you walk in a state of lack and you are continually walking in that fear of lack and never having, you are in lack and never having. But if you walk in that state of abundance, in that state of prosperity, you will always have prosperity. You will always have this amazing life, this life that is your birthright.

So, no, you don't have to be in a state of grace to create, but to be in a state of grace is to be present, is to be accountable, and is to be conscious of every part of your amazing life that you want to create. Sure, you can go back to the dead life that let life happen to you or you can rise up out of it and recognize the very moment the wave hits the shore, you have the whole beach to yourself to play, to build sandcastles, to do whatever you want, like a blank canvas of a painting. You see, it's blank, your life is blank and so every day it's like a brand new canvas of life. Create, change, do whatever it takes to make that life exactly as you want it and if you don't like that day, you need to know, that at the very moment that you don't want to be there, your canvas becomes clear and there is white again and you can be all back into the creative energy of creating your amazing life.

Q: "G", I'd like to go back to discussing chronic illness. When we talk about chronic illness, could you please bring clarity to me as to where alcoholism and drug addiction fall into this?

"G": Certainly. You see many diseases are based on your thoughts, your words, your feelings, your emotions and most of that can be cured by laying of hands or just falling into that place of faith. But with alcoholism and drug addiction, it's different and the reason it is different is because it is a disease of the soul, not just a disease of the human body. It is the one disease that can't be cured by someone else. It is a disease that transcends the physical and is one of the very few illnesses that affects the spirit.

Alcoholism, in the whole, has to do with being angry at God because of what has happened, angry at society or the world for something that may have been done. It can even be as simple as being angry at someone else. But because the soul is so powerful and resides in the heart, part of what happens is anger always resides in self and when you are angry at self to the point where you cannot forgive yourself, a lot of times people become alcoholic and it makes it easier to drink away self because then you don't have to be present in it. It removes you so from who you are that you get lost in the drugs and the alcohol and the disease takes over and all of a sudden you are lost.

Q: So, then is it fair to say that drug abuse and alcoholism disconnect you from your spirit?

"G": It is the one disease that disconnects you from what you would consider to be your God connection. It removes you from the very spirit. That is why, when people become deeply imbedded in alcoholism and disease like that, they sometimes cannot find their way out. The spirit is so suppressed and so far removed from where it belongs that it is painful for them to even cope with even their own existence.

Q: "G", depression is a really prevalent disease in our time and young children, even now seem to be affected and some even go towards suicide. What is bringing that about and what can we do?

"G": Very good. It's very difficult to be present in a life that you are so unhappy in, that you are so miserable in. So, depression removes you from the very present day life. You become lost in self, so to speak. In a society that is based on a religion that tells you that you are bad or a sinner or that you are continually bombarded with acts of being wrong, what else could you do, but fall away from your life, detach yourself to the point where you suppress your spirit and become depressed? Alcoholism, depression, mental illness, all these diseases are based out of a desire to be absent of now, absent of your life.

Q: What is the message that you would send out to people who have found themselves walking this journey to help them through it?

"G": The greatest message that I can give mankind is that if just one holds hope for all of mankind, just one, the ability to transform is a guarantee. You see, God has this soft spot for mankind that truly believes that just by the evolution, just by the journey, man can change. It wants to. I have seen it.

People are searching all the time. I hear people say "I want to have a personal relationship with God. I want to know God. I want to embrace God. I want God in my life." And what do you do? You look for him or her. You look for that evidence of God and what I can tell you is, God is present. God is right here, right now, in you. It is not to search outside, but to truly find, within yourself, the ability to reclaim your relationship and your connection to God. I have said many times before, that if you are present in every part of your life, if you capture one moment of your life and then another moment of your life and you place them side by side, they become the whole sum of one's life. Imagine having God in every part of that.

Think about disease as a whole, it is absence of light. It is dark. It is dense. It creates a hole, a separation, a suppression of some sort. But when you do what I just said, bring God into every moment of every cell of your being, darkness cannot be. Remember when I talked about a candle? If you had a candle in the center of the room, a small candle in the darkness, it dispels the dark. So, that's what you hold to. "G" holds that flame of light. "G" holds that flame of hope that dispels the darkness because every moment that you bring light into every moment or every cell of your being, it changes it, shifts it, moves it past.

Remember the woman with cancer? She walked fearless. Remember the journey of your life is about being fearless and facing your life with goodness and love. Know that God loves you. He loves you very, very much and He/She holds for you that which you sometimes feel you cannot. That is the blessing and that is the glory of the journey. That is that permanent state of grace.

Q: When the soul comes in and it has had other lifetimes where it has been suppressed, does it actually come in diseased and is this where the similarity in genes comes into the family of origin?

"G": It's interesting how man likes to fall on that whole concept that it runs genetically in families. What it really is, is lifetime after lifetime, you create karmic debt. You wrong someone, you come back and you pay it back. I talked about this in earlier segments of this series. Well, one of the things you have to remember is, karmic debt is your way of righting a wrong. So, if you come into this world with disease or illness, it could be karmic. It could be that there is something unfinished between the parents of the child or maybe there was something unfinished between one or two people in the journey. Either way, until man learns that they do not have to walk the road of karmic debt, it will never change. So, I am here to help you to rise up out of karmic debt, karmic loop, and move past it so that you walk debt free. How do you do that? By recognizing the mistake, recognizing the issue at hand, claiming in the present moment, right here and right now, that 'I proclaim my life and my life is a journey free to walk all the time in the light of God.' And when you do that, it removes you from those things that you seem to think you have to pay back.

You have to remember, man tends to create a whole lot of things to fix things, but it is very simple. All you have to do is claim your life, claim your birthright, and the moment you claim the original birthright of who you are, all karmic debt is done. So, guess what? Claim your birthright. Walk the road of enlightenment. Be the light. Go forward. That will take you to that place of God realization. You won't have to search for it, you will be it.

The greatest thing I can teach each of you in this journey, if you can just for a moment get quiet and get out of the way, is quit carrying your backpack of suffering. Quit carrying the baggage that you seem to think was all about you. It's funny, man does that. Man carries, in the now, all the baggage of the past just in case they might need it. Well, when you are carrying the baggage of the past, you are really not in the moment, are you? You have this illusion that you think you are, but you are not, so backpacks off the back. You are walking debt free, you are walking karma free. Remember absolute absolution says you are forgiven before you have done it. Now that does not give you the right to wrong someone and just say "well I have absolute absolution." It does not work that way. Absolute absolution is when you recognize a mistake or a wrong that you have made and you recognize it and say "I am forgiven". It means going forward in the light of God, not with intention to hurt another person. That is the only way that absolution works. You have to walk in the light of God. That way it is done.

God Realization

We have no idea what we are.
We continue to try and fit into the ordinary
Because we fear the Light inside.
What if someone sees the true indwelling God?

Now I ask, "Consider what the prophets have done?"
Some hold within them the fire.
Some speak to the ocean of life and reflect.
Some formed and wielded steel of creation.
Some ride the winds to find self discovery.

Go forward on this journey
Walking invisible with the masters.
For they do not seek fame and glory.
Only the quiet walk of enlightenment,
And the love of fulfillment,
As they continue to expand the consciousness of the human race.

God realization is the continuous illumination of the self realized life. In order to become what we already are, we spend the moment being us.

In the beginning, we were aware of our existence. Our uniqueness was our point of origin. And soon after our birth, we began to move further and further away from what we knew to be our true essence. We began to complicate the road by taking it apart, compartmentalizing our existence. We began to lose the priority of the journey. We began to recognize the needs, the wants, the must haves.

We began to go to a place that was void of one thing - the true essence of God. We fell away from our uniqueness and started to become a copy of each other.

Pretty soon we began to stop thinking for ourselves. We stopped being unique. We lost harmony. We lost the sound of God. We began to lose interest. It became very apparent that for a long time the very road we desired was the road we ran from. Instead of being unique in our own understanding, we began to fill it up with other people's stuff.

To really find the journey, to really know the journey, means being the absolute state of who we are - claiming our birthright, being the energy of God, being the intention of the road, being in the now, in the moment and finally, being fully God realized.

Someone once said to me, "I believe in you." What was hard in the beginning was that I didn't believe in me, and in order to come to God realized, I had to believe, I had to take a leap of faith. I had to have a sense of knowing.

I truly struggled for a long time because my understanding of God realization was a yogi master who walks the life, figuring it out, being in meditation all day long. I even believed that a master would perform laying on of hands and heal instantly. Those would be God realized individuals.

Then I look at me and my life. At first, I couldn't even pull a rabbit out of my hat. I couldn't get out of being lost in the rhymes of my own failures in life. I continually cycled in and out, thinking that God realization would never be possible. What I learned on this journey is that I am my true self when I recognize the true you, for we are God realized. "G" once said, "*Divinity is not about being out there and greater, but being in the heart and within reach."* That is being God realized.

So the question is, "How does one get to a place of being God realized?" It begins by looking at our life, the things that we've experienced. There comes a point in a person's journey when we must make a decision about our life.

I wrote the following at a time when I was trying to figure out who the real God realized person was inside of me. I struggled with the person that I believed I was because I thought I would never fit my image of a God realized master.

I wasn't aware that every day, as I come into my life, I'm like a new arrival starting each day, brand new:

Am I joy?
Am I depressed?
Am I happy?
Am I mean?
Am I fearful?
Am I angry?
Am I prosperous?
Am I lacking?
Am I oneness?

I realized that I must welcome and attend to all of them.
Even as sorrow sweeps into my life,
I must treat it with honor,
For it just may be the turning point in my path.

I had to learn to wake up to the delights of change
And embrace the moment.
If I accept what troubles me,
I know it opens the door that I have been beating on my whole life.
What do I mean by that?

It means that each thing I have fought against
Has been the very thing that changed me.
Each one brought me here
And that was human condition.

I have learned to welcome difficulty.
Once I have accepted it,
I can see the journey of human condition and human factor
As old worn out clothes that at one time had served me well.
Now I see them off me.
I undressed this human being called me
And began to see the true beauty of the naked spirit.

The sweetness of life, free and powerful,
Helped me to forge ahead with such healing
That I set out on the enlightened road.
I am thankful for I had to learn to praise this life.
It has taught the master in me.
It became the union of God within me.

I now see that God holds the secret cup
That helps us through the long nights when we think we are alone.
I have learned through meditation
That I have known before the beginning of this universe
That we are walking in this life waiting.
It is time to push through
To the master that I know lies within.

Someone once asked "G" the question, "How do we become God realized if we are so imperfect?" "G" replied, "God realized masters are not perfect. They recognize their imperfections, embrace them, do what they can to change them, and move on."

The journey to become God realized begins with finding self. We look for God outside of ourselves because we are afraid to look at what's inside. We feel worthless, undeserving of a loving life of God.

My idea of God realized is to truly do a deep soul search to figure out exactly who I am and not to find my reason for being here because I already know that. That sounds kind of egotistical, but it's not like I'm out there running people down with my life. What I am doing is more like witnessing my life and making conscious choices to be more present in what I do instead of letting things happen to me.

An example would be that for most of my adult life, I have been letting life come at me. I wasn't meeting my life head on. It was more like life was just happening to me. I wasn't directing it, consciously doing things to make my life better. I would react more than I would create it, direct it.

My grandfather was so God realized, people would show up at the door and do the bible thumping thing and he would look at them and say 'no'. It wasn't out of fear, but what he knew. He had seen a lot of things growing up with his mother being a channeler, and he always had an open mind to this stuff.

He never fit the familiar role of religion. He was always fighting it, almost as though he challenged it at every corner. I really admired him for his tenacity, his strength, his conviction and what he believed. He wasn't afraid of the bible. He had one. To him, it was all just a bunch of words. I think that's where I got the idea that man fills himself up with too much stuff. I heard it from him and "G", too.

He was never a victim. He was a rock. I never knew my grandfather to be run down or run over. Most of the time, for him, he really wore his life well. What I realized was that what was missing more than anything was real compassion for himself. He wore kind of an iron facade. He had an energy about him that caused people to be afraid of him, but I think he did that because he was not one to let people get too close. Even though he was very quiet around them, when he spoke, people would stop and listen. But when I had him, he was talking to me all the time. My grandmother once said she couldn't believe how much he talked to me. I would ask him questions. He would pretend to be irritated, but then soften up and answer.

There was physical and mental abuse, alcohol abuse, a lot of things in my home. My grandfather would take me and my cousin because of the alcoholism that was so prevalent in my parents. It was a safe haven for us.

He taught me not to just accept things when they came. He said if it didn't resonate with me, I needed to get up and leave. You don't know how many times we would get up and leave a church service because nothing was happening in his heart. I kind of became a gypsy church goer. I learned that God really wasn't the building or the words. I learned that God was in nature, in the animals, in our heart.

I remember once we were sitting in the back yard. There was a squirrel that lived in the big tree, and he would come up and eat from grandfather's hand. He said to me when I was really little, "This is where you will find God." I watched him. He would hand the squirrel nuts and it would be happy and run off to hide them.

My grandfather always said the real essence of God was in everything and every body. God is not a thing. God is a feeling.

I was nine years old when I learned all this. I had a couple of profound years with my grandfather. Those two years instilled some strong beliefs in me: don't settle, listen to the heart and know that God is within.

When he died, my parents lied to me. I was and am psychic. On the night of his passing, when he was in the hospital, he came to me and told me that he was going away. I asked if I could go with him and he told me no. Yet the adults lied to me when I asked if my Grandfather had died. I knew I couldn't trust them or anything they said to me.

Grandfather was the strength and now that he was gone, that was gone. I lost hope. I couldn't understand why this God of love that he had told me about would take him away from me. I started to blame God.

It was like the further away from his death that I got, the more I lost hope because it was so final. I knew I would never see him again. During my youth, due to the alcoholism in my family, there was no one else that was that spiritual light. I did have spirit guides named Michael and Jonathan that I communicated with, but they weren't in the flesh. And they weren't accepted as real by anyone around me. I felt really lost for a long time. It was like wandering aimlessly through the desert looking for an oasis.

I started searching for God again when I was sixteen. That was about the time my mother sobered up and began her own spiritual journey. I remember what my Grandfather had taught me. I think it's what made me hop from church to church. I tried to get back the same feeling of God in my heart that I had when I was a kid. I'd had the feeling, but had lost it. I lost it because I got lost in the human chaos, the human condition, the mundane things in my life.

We can never unknow what we know, but we can bury it, we can put stuff on top of it. Like when we have stuff in our house, the more stuff we have, the more we can't find. That's kind of what I did. I filled my spiritual house with a lot of rules, church stuff, Christianity, Judaism. My mother wasn't a church goer, but she had me going to a Lutheran church where we got confirmed and baptized. At that point, I didn't like the Lutheran church because it was confining. I had a friend who was a born again Christian, and she pushed a new church. I went to that for a while and then tried a Baptist church for a while. Eventually religion left a bad taste in my mouth and I stopped attending altogether. I then turned to drugs and alcohol. That didn't work either.

When I sobered up in my early twenties and had to look at my life, I realized there wasn't much there. The drugs and alcohol had been to replace all that I had lost when my grandfather died. Between my father's and my mother's alcohol abuse and the abuse growing up, it was like, in some way, I had died inside. Even after going through treatment, I hooked up with a very abusive man for a very long time, so the abuse continued.

It wasn't until much later, in my late twenties, that my husband and I had gotten counseling for the abuse. So that stopped, but I never really found me. I had allowed the life to be beaten out of me. I was just existing, not alive, not dead, just existing. "G" would call that the walking dead.

It was in this part of the journey that one day I looked in the mirror and realized I didn't want to live like this anymore. I started to find myself and I started looking for God again.

I wasn't sure where I would find Him, but I started looking under every rock, behind every bush, and I returned to church hopping like I did with my grandfather. I found myself trying to find God again, to put myself back together.

There was a very dear friend who had been listening to a woman motivational speaker. My friend had been trying to get me to go and see her and finally one day I went. I walked through the doors and saw a woman who couldn't have been more than 5'1", red hair, spiked heels, and in her sixties at the time. She didn't fit the image of what I was expecting. She was fiery, fearless and pretty much took on anybody. The first thing she said to me was, "You are the cause and affect of your entire life and if you don't like what's happening, you need to stop pissing and moaning and start doing something about it."

I looked at my friend and thought, "What the hell have you brought me to?" What was interesting is that I went for three years. It was pretty empowering because the woman woke me up to my life. I could feel God in her. I couldn't feel it in me, but I could feel it in her and I was drawn to that. What I have learned is that if we are not being fed more and more information, we pull away and start to look again. I had learned as much as I could from her.

I had forgotten the words my grandfather had told me a long time ago, "God is a feeling inside you, in your heart." I started to search, but everywhere I went, it was the same stuff. It was all good, but I hungered for more. My spirit was starving for it. I wanted to fill it up and I didn't know how to go about doing that.

Something inside of me kept me going. I kept hearing, inside myself, the voice of my spirit and my grandfather urging me on. I kept feeling this pull to keep going and to keep the momentum happening. The knowing kept getting stronger and the further down the road I got, the stronger the knowing got.

I had an out-of-body experience during a time when I was having a procedure done in the hospital. I was 36. I felt a true love from this being of light that came to me and for the first time since I was a child, I got that feeling of God back in my heart. I didn't know it then, but it was the first time I met "G".

At this point, I had started looking in all different places and I found a woman who channeled the Christo energy at an event called the 12:12. The year before that, I had been told by my guide, Jonathan that I would be bringing in a new kind of energy. Being a psychic intuitive and listening to spirit for most of my life, I knew that when they said stuff, it usually came true. I just didn't know how or when it would. It was at this event that I became a full body channel for "G".

I have channeled "G" now for 13 years. He has encouraged me to find myself, my own true essence, my spirit. He has always supported me, never judged me and always loved me, no matter what. However, I can't say that of my family. This has been a very difficult road for them as well as me. As I became more sure and stronger in my journey, it made them more uncomfortable because it identified in them their own insecurities in the road. I eventually realized that my husband and I had grown apart and that we were not seeing the same vision ahead. Because of that, we began to create a lot of conflict in our relationship. He's not a bad person and I'm not a bad person; we just aren't good together now and have divorced. Did my spirituality cause this? No. It's because I've finally learned who the real Lynn is and have begun to let her out. There is a point in all of this where I finally came to a realization that when I was sitting in my life and feeling stagnant, not because of the other person, but because I was holding myself back out of fear of rejection, that's what spurred me on. I hadn't been allowing myself to be who I really was.

Now all of this happened to be my journey. One doesn't need to be in abuse, on alcohol or drugs, or in any bad situation to be God realized. It is just coming to a realization of uncovering what the real spirit is all about. I realized that I was looking for God outside of me, not inside of me, and that was part of why I was still searching.

As I talk to others on the road, I am finding similar truths. There is an innate desire in the spirit to connect back with God, not just connect with God, but truly commune with God. It's having a personal love affair with God.

So, what's it like communing with God? What do I mean by that? I mean that I recognize the wisdom I have within and I feel deep inside, a true love for my life and a true love for the people around me. It's not the human love of conditions and expectations; it's an unconditional love, an accepting love that transcends the emptiness that I felt in the past.

I see the God light in other people all the time now. The knowing I am uncovering is also the God within. When I ask questions, I get answers, and that is the God within. I used to ask a question and I wouldn't get an answer. Now it's instantaneous.

What changed that? I'm not questioning me like I used to. I have come full circle in acceptance of myself and the road. The deeper I know me, the true me, the more knowing I have, the more connected I feel. I can feel the divine master within and know that is who I am connecting with and walking this road with.

When I connected with my master self and allowed that connection to be, it opened a door to me that I had craved for so long that I was like a beggar. I so badly wanted it, but couldn't find it. But when I did find it, I didn't have to worry about taking it or stealing it, because it was like my cup runneth over with information.

It's interesting that now when I work with clients I have greater clarity than I have ever had. I can talk to dead people, but what has happened is that people need validation and confirmation. That's what they are looking for when they want to talk to dead relatives. They want tangible proof that it exists. People want to talk to their relatives on the other side, but rarely do they ask them what God is like. It gets back to the fear of God. They think religion has taught them so well that they don't even need to ask.

I really feel that the real connection to God is feeling awake. It's not the kind of awake in the human sense, but greater than that. It's feeling awake in the spirit that says,

"I'm alive! I'm here! I'm present and I'm ready to work or do what I desire to do or am ready to be."

A lot of the people in the "G" channeling groups who have come to me in the past several months have said how much their lives have changed as a result of what they are learning. They are finally recognizing their accountability in the journey. It's because they have become consciously aware of themselves and their road. It is amazing to watch. And it's amazing to me to know that somebody took it into their heart and went with it.

Being God realized is not like having to go out and blow a horn to say this is it. It's not like having to go out and scream or shout, "I'm God realized." It's private. It's subtle; it's like a secret that we have with God. One of the things I learned from the Masters of God Consciousness that I work with is, it's not like they have to tell us who they are, they just know.

Somebody asked me recently if I was God realized. I wasn't sure how to respond. I wanted to tell them that it's a secret or that it is something you have to figure out. Instead I flat out denied it. When I did that, I took myself out of God realization altogether. I back pedaled, got into doubt. I threw a veil over my head and the veil I am referring to is not the one we get married in. The veil I am talking about is the veil of human condition and the veil of unworthiness which is a part of human condition.

We have been taught for so long that if we admit that we are God realized, it's ego, or blasphemy. That's not what it is. We know we have been with someone who is God realized when we walk away and we have either a huge 'aha' or our own personal awakening from the experience.

I believe that the awakening of God realization is to raise the consciousness of the planet, to raise the awareness of man and woman. However, it scares the crap out of people and they don't want to be God realized, or if they say they do they don't do the legwork to get there, because it means accountability and accountability for our whole life is scary. There's no one to blame for our life being the way it is, but us. I could go back and blame my parents, my husband, etc for my life, but I can't do that anymore. I am awake. I am aware and the only place to go now is forward.

What I am learning is that I just have to be me, my own light in my own space and hold my part of the puzzle of life. And if by some chance somebody meets me on the road or meets me in a store or reads this book or talks to me, if I can emulate that God light, that place of knowing, and I change somebody because of that, give them an 'aha' or awaken them in some way, I will know I have done my part. It can be something as small as being kind to someone or listening when they need someone, or as big as an auditorium full of people coming to hear "G" speak.

It took me several years, but I finally came to the realization that God is in everything. It was not in the church where I found Him. I had to find Him in me. I had to find my personal, indwelling, loving God within. That was it in itself, and the only way to do that was to find a love of self. I had to stop beating myself up for the mistakes I had made in life. I had to stop beating myself up for what I did, said, or acted. I had to finally come back to the realization that when I found me, I would find God. That's really what it came down to.

"G" has always said, *"God is within you. You are co-creators with God, made in image and likeness of."* What I realized was that "G" had been telling us all along that when we stop hating who we are and love who we are, and when we stop trying to be for someone else, is when we finally become really present in our life, really in our life. It's not external anymore, it's internal.

When I became aware of me, became conscious of my life and intentionally walked in a specific direction, that was when I could truly embrace the indwelling God.

It has been for me a real awakening over the last several years because now I am very aware of who I am and what my direction is. I am not floundering anymore. I am able to get past the uncertainty. I used to be uncertain all the time. As time goes by, the uncertainty has been abating. I am slowly arising to a knowing now; I just know what I know. Somebody asked me, "How to you know?" I just know. It's like the journey has unlocked the knowledge.

I am not here to convince you that what I say is the truth. You will come to your own conclusions in the journey. It usually starts with a knowing in your heart. If what I say resonates with you, you will take it into your heart. I am just here to be a witness to my life, a witness to the journey and a witness to God. My journey is to teach when people are ready to hear it. My journey is to be the light when there is great darkness. My journey is about walking in God realization and recognizing the God in everyone.

Channeling by "G"
"God Realization"

Note: The following text is transcribed from an actual channeling by "G". The content and grammar is written as spoken by "G".

"G": Hello, this is G. Tonight we are going to talk about God realization. It is through this book that we have discovered the journey of birthright and the energy that commands it. It is through that experience we have come to understand the intention of the road and that all creation is in the moment now. Now it is time to recognize the journey of self realization and move into finding our God realized life.

"G": Hello everyone.
All: Hello "G".

"G": Welcome tonight to this section on God realization. In the last four sessions, we have talked about birthright, which is your right to all existence, to the power of God to co-create, to unconditional love, to absolute absolution, which then leads us to an understanding of the existence of man, the energy of how man came to be.

Now, all of man is on the journey to find themselves. They look for something. They say "I need to find me." You know I have heard people say, "Why am I here? What is my purpose in life? What is the journey all about?" And I bet everyone in this room has even said that, yes? So, you see, it is a part of the basic human nature to do that, to question, to ask "Why, why, how come?" You do that and it is interesting because the question 'why?' leads you to the next level, to the next road, maybe to the next understanding in your life. Like I have said before, to become God realized, you must first become self realized and that means acceptance, that means honor.

Well somewhere in the journey of this creation, man lost their connection to God, or they thought they did, and so became the journey of separation and this place of duality and loss. So, in this place of man's discovering of duality, it began a journey of moving further and further and further away from the true existence of their birth, their true birthright. See, man forgets that they were created in image and likeness of. And see, when you lose that, all of a sudden you become isolated, alone, lost, searching, wondering and that is why man has looked for God outside. Somewhere out there, God is watching, somewhere out there God knows.

Well, the true understanding of God is within. God is not placed somewhere out there, He is placed within you. That is yours, your little piece of creation built right inside and it sits there waiting for you to command it, direct it, create with it, even when you don't think you are creating. Like I have said in earlier sessions, words, thoughts, feelings, and emotions create, and when you are in that part of creation, it is fast, very fast. It is time that man and woman come back full circle and no longer see themselves as separate from, but being a part of, being the whole of their life, the whole of their existence.

There are many masters that walk this earth and have come here God realized. What happens in a God realized life is man no longer has the desire to search outside, but to look within. What that does is it brings them closer to the God they crave, the God that they desire to know. So, you see, if you go in, you find God waiting. That is part of the true essence of waking up and finding what really is yours. Everyone in this room and on this planet has a piece of creation that is specifically assigned to them, and that very small part, which is actually quite huge, but small in the essence of the All, this piece, when you look inside of it and truly embrace the understanding of it, is so big that most people run from it. That is part of why man has had such a difficult time finding the God within because it is so huge to them and it frightens them.

I have heard master after master. I have seen so much. One of the greatest masters that ever walked said "Fall into your master self and expand." Now that statement alone is so big that it would take a whole quarter in college just to figure out what it means. There are people who will sit and dissect and break down just that statement alone. So you have to understand that these parts, these things that you seek to find, are not out there somewhere, but in here somewhere.

Q: "G", what is the master self?

"G": Very good. The master self. You have to understand that spirit has many levels and what that is. This body is a very dense form. You know you touch and it is very dense and very firm, but as energy rises it gets lighter and lighter and lighter. The master higher self is the divine spirit. This is the spirit in which you exist. It is the whole of your existence. Remember how I talked about how we had Pitch and Hue, Light and Sound, that kind of thing? Well, they reside in those spaces and those energies are like the highest form of your God realized self. That part of the master self is that spirit's will that knows your answers, and knows what is best for you. It knows the road that you are going to walk and how to achieve it to its highest level. The master self is your merging with your divine spirit. Your master self is the master walking the master path.

Q: "G", can you guide me as to how to bring in my master self?

"G": I will give you some steps. When someone is searching for God, it immediately takes you out of the equation, so stop searching because God is not out, It is in. So, instead of searching for God, claim God. Call It in and say "I claim the God within." That is the first step in becoming God realized, because once you accept the God inside, the true indwelling spirit of God, there is no wavering. Someone can come to you and you would not waver in the road because you know in the very moment of meeting that person, that they have their God within and that is who you can communicate with, connect to. It does not take you away from, but brings you closer to God instead of pushing you away.

The true essence of the indwelling God is to give you, what I call, the very bilingual soul, so that you can be wherever it is in the road and journey and be able to speak whatever language there is. And I'm not talking language like Spanish or whatever. I am talking about soul to soul, heart to heart. So, if you are asking how do you get there, stop searching for God outside. Look within, that is the first step.

Once you have claimed the God within, the second step in all of this is there are moments when you will fall away because it's an old pattern. It's easy to fall away and to forget what it is that brought you there in the first place. You know, somebody once said, ""G", you know I come and I be with you and I am so God realized when I am in the energy and I walk out that door and I just get blasted with something and I fall out of it." And he said, "I can't walk with my eyes closed; it doesn't work very well." And I said to him, "You have to understand that being out of it is just a reminder of how much you really want it, so it's not a negative. What it does is give you that moment to say, "Yes,

I desire a God realized life, and it is mine now." And when you claim that, less and less do you have those experiences of falling out of God. So, it's practice. Like I always say, practice makes perfect.

What I wanted to explain to you is to fall into your master self. Many of the students that have come to see "G" are learning the advanced master journey and part of that is learning to bring the higher master self in. It is interesting to talk to the students because every one of them, even if they have not talked to each other, have the same experience when their master self comes in and that is the quieting of the mind, the slowing of the heart. That is the two similarities that they have. Now of course people feel other experiences in the journey, but those are the two things that are symbiant and absolute in every experience that they have had. Part of that coming in, the quieting of the mind....see the mind, that's that duality stuff. The mind will talk you in and out of stuff. You know you fall out of God, fall back into God, that's the mind stuff. And when you become and fall into your master self and allow the master to merge with you, what happens in that very moment is that the mind no longer has control. Now, you have just placed your master self in the driver's seat of your own destiny.

Q: "G", how do I know I am bringing in my true master self rather than some other energy?

"G": Well the first thing I teach my students is that they ask that only birth light or God light energy come in. That eliminates any negative or unwanted entities or energies that can come forward. The second thing I have them do is I have them get very quiet, like you do in meditation, and you ask your master self to step forward. Once that master self steps forward, that is where you will notice the quieting of the mind. There is also a slowing of the heart, but each person has their own experience with bringing in their own master energy.

One of the things that I would like to explain is that master energy, when you are working with it or bringing it in or whatever you may be doing with it - when you are working at this level and doing this journey, you need to be very prepared and also be educated on the process of how to do it so that when you do it, you have the enlightenment and knowing that what you are doing is correct. I would not recommend this for just anyone because you do not want to do something when you have not practiced. Many of my students have been studying for several years before they actually attempt to do this.

As a beginner, you can work in meditation with your master higher self. You can work with just feeling the energy of the master higher self, and maybe getting answers in meditation with the master higher self. That will help guide you in your life. That is what they are here to do, to help you find that road of being God realized. So, I recommend that people practice in meditation and things like that, but overall you really need to take the time and be educated in the journey. Some of my students now have their full master energy in body and can walk and talk and so it is quite fun to watch them as they expand and grow and come into God realization. The goal in all of this is to help mankind to bring that forward. Because of all that is happening in this world, the more masters that walk the road and are in God realization, the faster the planet will evolve and heal in this journey.

Q: What happens with the brilliance of a person when they have these aha's? Are they in contact with their master self?

"G": So, think about when you are having those moments you call aha's or those realizations that come like when you go, "Oh, I understand this", and you don't know why but all of a sudden you have this instant clarity. Your master self is never very far from you. It can't be, it's right there all the time and it is in that place where you have these glimmers because they will tap into you like a little finger that touches you and says "here it is" and you might get this moment of clarity that says "Oh, now I understand". It is then when you hear that or know that, yes, that is being in contact with the master within. That does not mean the master resides within, but they are always connected to you.

The goal of this journey is to be God realized. You know masters walk this planet and many that have come here enlightened. This road of enlightenment is the quiet journey of enlightenment. That is why the mind quiets. You know when you are sitting there bringing the master selves in and the mind quiets, it is because enlightenment is not silent, but it is quiet. In the quiet is where you see and experience and learn the things that you need to help you on the next turn in the road.

Q: So, "G" why have we in this world gotten so busy and so not quiet?

"G": That is a question I have been asked many, many times in the journey. In the last fourteen years since I came to help mankind to find themselves, man's rushing seems to be the only answer they have to everything. They try to fit the whole of their life in one day. You can't fit the whole of your life in one day. What you need to do is be present in your life and allow what it is, allow its best qualities to unfold. The quality of your life is greater when you are fully immersed in the knowing of you. See, people tend to be external and outside of self.

I was having a conversation with somebody just today and I was looking out and I saw cars go and go and people go and I said, "They are rushing to nowhere" and the person I was sitting with said, "It's like they are rushing to fill up space, to fill up their life with things that are important, G." And I said, "Ah". The interesting thing is, why would you rush to fill up what is so beautiful? Why would you rush your life to fill it up with all the things that mean nothing that you can't take with you? Do you know what you take with you in your journey? You take all the experience of love, the sunrise, the sunset, the smile, the touch. You don't take the busy of the day, the car rushing around. You don't take that with you because that's not important. What is important is to truly find, in this very beautiful life, all the color, all the love, all the acceptance, all the beautiful things that your spirit holds.

Has anyone ever sat and really watched a bumblebee? Most people will watch them for a while, but then they get this fear going and really get away from them fast. But you see, I have sat and watched a bumblebee and it's very interesting. Do you know that when the bee was created, the true theory is that the bumblebee's wings are not big enough to sustain its weight. Well think about that. But see, the little bumblebee did not hear that. It did not hear that it couldn't fly. What it knew is that it was going to fly and it went against the whole rules of nature and said "I'm flying." So, what happened is even though the wings were very small, they just went a little bit faster and it was because of that speed that the bee could do the impossible.

But you see, the bee has a mission. His job is to take himself from one flower to the next and his job, though he is unaware of it, is to pollinate different flowers. Now it thinks that its job is to collect this pollen and this nectar and take it back and it creates honey so it can have more bees to do the job. But see, it's funny, even in it's unawareness it is doing something and it doesn't miss a hit. It goes from flower to flower to flower, but even though it is so busy in its day, busy, busy, busy, it is still creating beauty all around it.

Now you see, that is what man does: rushes along doing, doing, doing. He is still creating all the beauty around him, but he is missing it. It is truly missing the beauty being creating. It's time to turn around. I have told the story about many people…you know when you have beliefs and journeys and stuff and everyone has their understanding, their interpretation of what they believe God to be….and it's interesting.

I told the story shared by an old prophet from a long time ago. What the story is, is that there were many people chained facing the wall in a cave and what they saw were dancing shadows on the wall. That was their life. That was what they believed their world to be. They said, "This is truth; this is the reality of life."

But something happened. Someone reached out and unlocked one lone person and turned him around. All of a sudden he saw masters dancing around the fire light and his reality was not the same anymore. Could you put that man back to face the wall and say this is the truth, when he knows that the moment he turned around his life changed forever? No, because you can't unknow what you know. Think about that. Think about this one person going back and saying, "You don't understand. This is not the reality. This is not the truth. There is something behind us." They all looked at him and said, "You're crazy." Others began to talk about locking him up because he was speaking against what they all believed to be the truth.

But see, because he turned around, something changed him within and he began to awaken. The words he had spoken, caused a ripple such that one by one they all turned around and everyone was awakened to consciousness. They all knew the truth now. The truth they believed, the illusion that they held to be what they thought was, was no longer their truth. Now they see a whole new world that did not exist before then. They became God realized the moment that they stepped out of that fear of staring at the shadows that danced on the wall and turned around for the first time and embraced, embraced the masters dancing around the firelight.

Q: So then is part of the trouble that the human race is having is making the leap from self realized to God realized? Is that when we come face to face with the master and we don't embrace it?

"G": Absolutely. It has been interesting because if you look throughout history, what have you done to your masters? You've killed them, you've shunned them, you've kicked them out of a country and you've banished them far away from the very people that loved them. See, mankind has lost something in the journey. They have lost the one thing that sustains them and that is wisdom. They have fallen away from their wisdom and have embraced ignorance. They embrace all those things that say "I know what's best." How do you know what's best? Do you know what's best for the person sitting next to you? You cannot, for you are not in their shoes and you are not living their life. A part of being God realized is accepting each and everyone's uniqueness and embracing it to its fullest. It's finally saying "I love you for you, not for changing you, but for you, your unique flavor. This part of you makes this part of the journey more flavorful, more beautiful."

Now you think about going down the road, walking in your life, and you meet someone. If you are so caught up in stuff, caught up in the busyness of the day, what happens? You miss the flavor, you miss the quality of that one human being that could have said something that would have transformed your life, but see, you are caught in the busyness of the day. Like the bumblebee who was busy, busy, busy collecting nectar, collecting all that it could, going back to make more honey so that they can make more bees. Truly it was missing its own creation, missing the opportunity of watching flowers unfold.

It is interesting, too, there is a double analogy to that. See, really, the bumblebee comes and does its thing and goes to the flower and goes to the next flower and next flower and then goes back to its life. The flower is God and the bee comes and brushes against one part and then moves to the next part and each time God expands, but the bee is unaware that it has helped God to expand, so, it is in a symbiant relationship.

What "G" would love for mankind is not to miss the unfolding of God because God is within you and if you miss the unfolding of God within, your life becomes a shadow and you watch the shadows on the wall again.

Q: "G", can you expand on that symbiant relationship and how we and all the plants and animals are symbiant with you?

"G": See all of energy cannot exist without the other. You know how you have oxygen, correct? And if you remove something from it, it cannot sustain life anymore, can it? What happens? It changes and is toxic. But you see, you can't remove the elements to make it any different. Just like God, you are all the elements of it, and without you having your belief, your journey, your life, God would not go on. You would not go on. Where you go, God goes. It is symbiant. Do you see what I am saying? There are animals created on this planet and there are bees and there are insects, correct? Now everybody doesn't know this, but in the rainforests of South America there is a frog, a little tiny frog. And by destroying the trees there, you are killing the only place in the world they exist. But you have to understand, when they die, they are a part of the next evolution. When you remove this little frog, which happens to be food for something else, or its relationship to something else grows because of its existence, what happens to existence when you remove one element out of it? It no longer can sustain life, just like oxygen cannot sustain you if you remove any part of it. When you put more carbon dioxide into the air or kill the trees so that trees can't make anymore, guess what? The symbiant relationship of the planet and you cannot be. The trees create oxygen for you, correct? And without you creating the carbon dioxide that they need to turn it around, guess what? You need each other. Together the planet has balance and just like all the animals, they all have their part in this. So, when you kill something to the point of its extinction, you are causing the extinction of man.

Q: Well, "G", given the state of affairs that mother earth finds herself in today, what is the role that human beings must play in order to turn this around? I have heard you say before that you hold divine hope. So help!

"G": Think of it like this. If you don't become aware and truly recognize your part in this journey of co-creation, and your part of changing this pattern in life, man will be gone. Now, I'm not saying it's hopeless, because I hold divine hope and I wouldn't be coming here if I didn't hold the idea that this could be turned around, but it is becoming aware and waking up to the level of God consciousness. It means that you now stand in that place of being God realized. You will walk in your life, walk in this journey, changing the face of the planet. I believe, and I know, that man...all it takes is to change the momentum of consciousness and you change the momentum of this planet. If you can pray over water and heal someone from sickness by laying on of hands, if you can do all these things, then you have to hold to the understanding that to become God realized, is to help the planet to reach its God consciousness awareness. When that happens all together, not one at a time, but all together, you can change the momentum of the planet. You can heal what has all been done and transform it because I know, in co-creation, the power of our words create and if you take hold of just a small part of that, you will change the whole.

Q: I was wondering...I guess I see this as being connected...that we seem to perceive our lives as being so busy and fraught with time constraints, busyness, and the need to consume to fill our lives. Being a consumer society, I was wondering how we can change that momentum.

"G": Very good. Here is the key to something. Like I told you, you had to become aware of it first. You had to recognize that you were not in the momentum of being God realized. And once you became aware of the fact that you were not in the momentum of that, you had to change it by doing things that would change that part of it. Like I said just a bit ago, I watched people rushing by and missing the whole of their lives. See, in spirit, time does not exist and I have said that before in other sessions. Time does not exist, yet you and God are co-existent. They cannot be separate. And if you truly stay present in the moment, you stop that word time completely. It was very interesting because someone had come to me and they were talking about how they could stop time, but they didn't know how they had done it. They asked, "Well how did I do that?" What's interesting is, to stay in the moment stops time.

Someone once came to "G" and said ""G", I'm late all the time." And I said "Well, first things first, you need to quit saying you're late all the time. Second of all, you need to stay present in the moment wherever you are and no matter what time, because time is a visual thing for this society, whatever time you leave, don't look at it. Don't go there in that place and have to see what time it is. Just know that you are in the perfect place at the perfect time. Isn't it funny? Because it is always in everything in man. When you are present in the now, in the moment, you just go."

She said "OK, I'll try that." So she left, got into her car and said, "Oh, God, I looked at the clock. OK, I'm in the moment, time does not exist, I'm in the moment." She put a CD in and it was funny because it was one that she had bought, a channeled session from "G", and she sat there listening to it. She was just driving, being in the moment, listening to what was being said, and all of a sudden she got to work, looked up and found she was on time. She went, "How did I do that?" That was because she stayed very present in the moment and did not go to that place of worrying about time.

As long as man stays in their God knowing, stays present in their life, stays here in your connection to all things, you have found it. If you see yourself as symbiant to God, that you are co-existent with God, that you are in alignment with God, that all things are you and God, that you are God realized, when you stay in that place of recognizing your power in the road, your ability to create all things in the moment is instantaneous. You take it to the next level of just quiet enlightenment which means being present in the moment and not racing through the day.

I know you are a consumer society. I know that you need more, need more, need more, but what do you need more of? More stuff to fill up the day so you don't have time to find God? Well, you do that just fine. Or maybe you simplify it. Maybe you let it go. Maybe you finally say to yourself, it's OK to have space, it's OK to not have it all full to the brim with stuff.

I always say simplify your life because the more you complicate it, the more you get lost in it, and the more you get lost in it, the more you can't find it, and when you can't find it, you go out and buy it to put it back in there anyway. So, the question is, simplify it so you know where everything is. That way you don't go out and buy the stuff you don't need. Right?

You have to recognize that in the journey of God realization, it just comes to a place of knowing. It's like you wake up one day and it's there. It's interesting because I have talked earlier in other sessions about how you have a level of awareness and a level of knowing, but something drives you to expand, something pushes you to the next level. You come up against a wall. Now you could do something, you could stop and just stay there and not have the desire to lift yourself up. But see, for someone who is really present in their life, there is a desire to have more, a desire to expand and they lift themselves up and push themselves over the side. They are just excited because there is more to know and once they reach that point where they have leaped over the wall, it's whole new journey for them.

It's interesting because most God realized people go to this place where they just seem to go and walk, just kind of be. It's like t give up their life for a while because they need to figure things out or be in that place. Do you know why most masters eventually will take, what they call, a time of quiet or maybe a sabbatical of sorts or a journey of walking the road for a while? It's because they know that they have spent a lifetime busy, they have spent a lifetime of filling it up with stuff. And all of a sudden, it means nothing to them. You can't take it with you. Yeah, it's nice to look at it, but what they discover is that, that does not make them.

What makes a God realized human is the expansion of learning. They walk out into the world and it's like for the first time, when you take a breath in, you truly feel the air move through your lungs and breathe out. You take another step and you feel your legs touch the ground and your foot impact as you walk, and then you take the next level of your journey and you say "look at what I see." But it isn't what you see out here because looking is only part of it. It's because the heart of God within is really beating for the first time. God is beating in your heart for the first time and all of a sudden nothing looks the same. You look out at life and you are so reverent of it. You look out into your life and you realize, in that very moment, that this is what it is about: it is about being awake; it is about being alive; and it is about taking in the essence and the smell of a beautiful flower.

It is the moment in which you take your life away and bring in your life. See, you have two of them. You have the life you live with other people and then you have the life of God and if you can push the life with other people out of the way long enough just to truly experience the life of God within, the rest of your life doesn't go away, it expands. It's like having it all, folks. Instead of picking and choosing and being so selective, it means having it all. It's having perfect health; it's having abundance; it's having all these things. And what's interesting, man is so desperate to have and yet does nothing, nothing to make it happen. They get busy. They get lost.

"G": Think about where you are, think about, really right now in this room the energy is really quite powerful and I have people falling asleep. Do you know why you're falling asleep. Because you're not ready to hear what I have to say. You're shutting down the energy because it scares the bejeesus out of you. So, I'm telling you, folks, that's how you know you're ready. If you can't stay conscious, if you feel yourself dragging down, if you're getting tired you're fighting the one thing that will bring you absolute joy, that will bring you absolutely everything that you desire in life. So, I don't look at it as bad, I just know that is where everybody is in the road. You know, you can't judge it, but it is an awakening and it is telling you. That is what happens. When you are sitting in a room with someone talking to you that is talking about enlightenment and you go ["G" made a snoring sound...], guess what? You're not ready. What that means is it scares you and your spirit says "Oh, I don't know if I'm ready for this...["G" dropped his head as if he was sleeping] and you shut down. So, ask yourself, "Why am I doing that? Why do I deny the very information that can take me to the next level in the road? Why do I do that? Why?" Well, I know why...because being God realized is not just accountability. Being God realized is the opportunity to walk in all, and to walk in all means to shed all that is familiar to you. It is to let go of all sickness, all lack, all of everything that you have ever created and truly walk the divine life. So, you need to ask yourself when you are sitting and if you have a hard time getting through this section of the book, you need to say, "Wow, I heard that. I've gotta do something about that." Yes?

Q: "G", is it that people don't want to hear about enlightenment because they think they would lose a self that they cherish or lose the self they think they are?

"G": What's interesting is they have already lost. That's the difference. When you get to that place where you aren't ready to hear it, you've already lost, folks. See, a master who walks in enlightenment walks in quiet contemplation. That does not mean that he doesn't speak. He talks a lot, but in quiet contemplation, he is able to go in and resolve whatever may be chaotic for him in the moment. A God realized master can walk into a room and calm it. He does not walk in and create more chaos. He knows that when he walks into that space, he holds the God light creation energy and he holds it to his heart, which is where God resides. And once he is there, once he is truly in that essence, people gravitate to him or they run away, depending on wherever they are in that.

Q: "G", as we discuss God realization, I wonder what you could speak to our youngest masters, the ones who are most God realized, our children. What is the message that you impart to them and that you want us to impart to them?

"G": One of the most important things that you have to understand is that the children of this planet are the future. And if you instill fear, doubt, uncertainty, or even if you tell them they cannot, that is what you create. But what I would like to see mankind do to these young masters that are walking in God realization is let them expand, allow them to grow, give them the tools they need to see all that they can. Don't limit their abilities. Show them infinite possibilities. You have to be the mirror. You have to be the candle and in that you will be that beacon for them. If you walk this road absolutely in your God realized self, you become the example for them so that they can move forward.

Children are your greatest teacher. If you watch them and how they deal with life in general, they truly teach you what it really is to be close to God. See, they have not forgotten. They know that they hold no anger. Have you ever noticed a child? They get into a fight and they are all fixed, but all the parents are fighting and they get mad for months, while the kids are only angry two, three minutes, half an hour, and the next thing you know they are out playing again. But adults don't do that. They don't let things lie. They hold a grudge, they hold it, it's so deep inside of themselves, it becomes like an ulcer in them.

So what I would like to see for the younger generation of the future God realized masters is that in this journey for them, that we hold every part of the gifts they bring to us. Hold them in reverence just like you would hold God in reverence. Hold yourself in reverence because they become the teacher as you become the teacher, for you are the student as they are the student, and together, when you are in this place of learning and expanding and growing, there is always, always this light that shines from you. So you be that light, be the candle in the mirror because I will tell you, if you are the reflection, the wind can't touch it, can it?

See, it's funny, when I first came, and it was a while ago, I was also in the expansion of learning the human part of it, how the body worked. You know, I would come through this channel and it would be like, "Oh, how do you get here. How to you get there?" I would look out and I would see they had candles in the room and I would look at them and I would see this light.

One of the greatest things that I remember teaching when I very first started was that the room itself, if you shut all the lights off and have one candle, small, lit in the room, the darkness is not dark. It warms with glow light and that glow light reaches to every corner so that it really dispels anything that is negative. So, that's why I say to you, when you are the candle and the light, you dispel the negative for it cannot be, it cannot reside in your space. I have said, "Negative cannot be in the light of God because it is absorbed back and it is pure again. "

So you remember this moment when you look at your children and your children do something that maybe you don't think is so good. Remember that in that very moment, it is just a moment, and you hold them, love them, teach them, but teach them with love.

It's funny, I was watching a young girl and she wasn't very old. I would say too young to have a small child, but she had one. She was pushing a cart and the baby was very upset, not very happy being in the cart. He was crying and you could see her frustration because the baby would not quit crying and out of that very moment she, I guess lost something, became angry and she struck the child. Now, you have to understand, it was not done out of a sense of a bad thing, it was a frustration. And of course the reaction by most people was bad, but see, "G" did not see that. What I saw was a very young girl taking on the role of something that was bigger than she was. Now, I could look at her and sit in judgment for her striking her child, but I also had to look at the fact that, out of the frustration of who she is, I knew just by being in her presence, being around her, I could feel her sadness because she did not want to hit the child. I knew that. So, it was in that moment that I did not judge her. I sent her absolute absolution. I forgave the moment because I knew that this too shall pass and she, in her moment, learned something very valuable. She looked up and she saw that somebody had seen her. She felt bad, and I approached her and said "It's OK" and I sent love to her. In that very moment, she cried.

You cannot look at somebody unless you truly know what is going on inside. That is why God does not judge for every part of your life is a learning experience, an opportunity to expand, to grow, to change something. Now, you could get into judgment and you could look at her and get mad. I have said many times, even in earlier parts of these sessions about how you are in your car, driving along, going pretty fast and someone cuts you off. You get angry and you get mad and just chase them down, and you want to give them 'the what for' just because you are in a bad mood too. But here's the thing, you don't know what has happened to the person in that other car. In that other car, may be a young mother who got a phone call that her three-year-old child is down with fever and is being rushed to the hospital because the child has slipped into a coma. You would not know that would you? So, how can you sit in judgment? How can you get angry at someone else when you do not know their story; you do not know who they are. Someone who walks in a God realized journey embraces the whole of a person's experience, looks at it and realizes in that very moment that this is their choice in the journey, their experience. Do I judge it? No. I cannot for do I have all that I know about it? No. See, it is difficult to make judgment when you truly do not know what really is and even if you knew, could you judge it? So, there you go.

It is important to recognize that the young ones look to you as the example in the road. What I would hope for masters walking a God realized life, masters or teachers or parents or whoever you are, would be to go out into the world and be the example of someone who is loving, unconditionally, someone who goes forth knowing that the co-creation of existence is based on a person's awareness and understanding. And when you look at these children, realize, realize with every part of your being that they are very old. When you look at them next time and they say something profound, you are going to go, "Oh, you're smart, you're wise."

What I would say to all masters walking a God realized life is that to be God realized, to really know the true essence of God is not to find separation of self realization, but to merge self and God into one, like a folding together. Self realization is really that part of God realization. See, what happens if you are clueless? What happens if you are sitting there and are put into a job that you know nothing about and I say, "Do this job?" Well, you would sit there for a while and probably spin and freak out and do wrong things and make mistakes and screw this up and then all of a sudden something happens that you do something and you go, "Oh, it worked" and all of a sudden you go, "Oh, I did one thing right. That's good." Then you go along and make some more mistakes and you screw it up and boom, you do two things right. And all of a sudden you go, "Oh, I did two things right" and then you go along and make some more mistakes and you fall down and pick yourself up and all of a sudden you make two more right. Now you have four so you see what you are doing? What you are really doing is raising and elevating yourself to the next level each time you find something and do it right. I don't see mistakes as mistakes. I see them as opportunities to expand so you just did a whole lot of expanding is what you did and that is very good.

Q: "G", as you are inside of us, you are seen. What about when you are invisible. What is the relationship like of the as-above-so-below?

"G": Oh, very good. I have said for a long time that heaven and earth are so close that it is like a marriage of two, that heaven and earth are becoming one, that they are no longer so far apart that they cannot touch. That is part of why more and more people are coming to enlightenment, why more and more people are coming to God realization in the journey. This is because the veil of heaven and earth is very thin and every year it gets thinner and thinner. It is a part of going to the next level, turning the next corner and there it is. Heaven and earth are one. They meet and become one in the very moment where masters of heaven and masters of earth become one and all of a sudden you are living it, you are being it. That is why I say to you, bring your higher master self in. That is heaven, and let it merge with the masters of earth. Together they are all one.

Q: "G", when that takes place, when that merge with the heavens takes place with the individual, is there any loss of individuality or our unique soul energy?

"G": Oh, very good. Actually, no. See how it works is the masters of heaven usually have not got a whole lot of understanding about down here and you down here don't have a whole lot of understanding of what's up there because you both forgot. So, what happens when you bring them together and you merge them together? You become even greater, even better. It's like it enhances the physical earth and it enhances the heavenly God. And all of a sudden, you are walking, all the time aware, not just at a limited knowing, but thousands and thousands of years of knowledge is set free and you are walking in that place, knowing exactly what it is and knowing exactly how to be. What happens is the birthright of man and the birthright of heaven are no longer separate and all of a sudden you have the energy of God and the unique soul energy as one. Then the true intention and focused intention come together and become one, and then all of a sudden all of this comes together in the moment of now. And when that happens, when that finally reaches its point where you are walking that way, God realization is no longer a dream. God realization is you: walking, breathing, God inspired, God knowing, God realized.

  This is what I will bring and help man to uncover in the journey. You have to do the legwork. You have heard this from many people on the planet, many masters have come and talked to you. What you have to realize is the biggest thing that has happened is masters have come and given information but they haven't given you the how. I am giving you the how. I will teach you how to walk God inspired, God realized now.

Q: "G", I was taught by a previous eastern master that I am supposed to serve others before my self in order to achieve God realization. However, I had not achieved for myself self realization as yet so I was giving myself away and eventually becoming resentful. Can you talk about taking the easier, softer path instead of a path of suffering which I had been taught was the nature of finding God realization?

"G": Oh, yes. There have been many masters who have fallen under the pretext that it is your lot in life to serve mankind and to give it all up and to go without because how could you possibly be God realized? Well, God is all things, God is abundance, God is all these things so you can have it all. See, the journey is about finding out who you are and finding your personal self. Know who you are. You can't go out into the world and help someone when you don't even know who the heck you are. How do you do that? See, did not the creation of man come from a sense of desire to learn, to expand, and to grow? That is how God became realized, how God became aware of Itself because It needed to expand, It needed to learn and grow just like mankind has needed to learn and grow.

So, you see, when people teach you that you must suffer, that it is your lot in life, that is coming from a sense of lack. God is not lack. God is not less. God is more. God is all. So, why would you go into the world of life teaching people to suffer? That is what you do. "You have to go the road in order to be enlightened." Well, let me tell you something: enlightenment doesn't come based on dollars. Enlightenment comes based on personal experience and personal expansion. It does not have to do with being poor and taking the suffered road. It means taking the road that has the greatest teacher. Rise above it and teach others to rise up and meet their God realized self. That is what it is about. It is not to take away, but to give you all.

The Journey Home
by Lynn Young

*I remembered the pain of suffering and I remembered it well.
It could be a good teacher if I am a good student.
What I forget is the knowing of the road.
We walk roads all the time, taking detours, roundabouts,
Side streets or the direct way in the journey.*

*I seem to see no way out; no cure for this suffering.
What am I reflecting into me?*

*I fell to the ground and wept for I could not see.
I yelled, "Why me God?" Am I not good enough?
Am I not strong enough?
Please God take this pain from me."*

*I heard the soft gentle words.
"I send you love. God's love."*

*It was then that I felt this power wash over me and into me.
I felt it deflect the pain, this suffering that I had chosen.
I realized that I was free in this journey of suffering.
I was now being cleared of my fear.*

*I began to see that God had not forsaken me.
I had forgotten about him.*

Just then I knew I was leaving the old way of my life,
To the place of my birth called unconditional love.

As I began to take in the power of love,
I could feel the night ocean fill with glints of light.
I found myself between heaven and earth,
This place where God plays.
I desire the truth of the universe.
I saw I knew nothing
for I was standing in the way of God's truth.

Is this enough?
For I am leaving this place of know-it-all,
To the place of knowing myself.

I see the circle of my journey.
Can I stop this movement of repeating patterns of my life?
Or am I again struck down by the rhymes of failure?
Just then as I was spinning again out of control.
The wind began to blow; the rain began to fall,
And I was just about to cry out again
When I saw a man standing before me.
He stood with arms stretched out.
I was wet and cold. He put his arm around me.
When I looked into his eyes, I saw God's love reflected there.
He then led me to a door and said,
"Open the door child; walk through to your true life."

I was touched by his kindness
And just as I was to thank him, he said;
"A beginning of your life without any inclination to end!"

What did it all mean?
Then like a wave of water washing over me,
I knew, life is a cycle that is continually moving.
As we move into our life, we begin it all over again, everyday.

*I could fall into my life, unaware of me,
Or choose to walk through life conscious of everything.*

*Just as quickly, I knew I was standing next to a master.
I fell to his feet and understood;
For he was showing me the way to my life.*

*I am on the winding road of my journey.
I was given the union of my soul spirit.
Now my soul and spirit walk as one in the grace of love.
The strength of God
to see that we both arrive together as one, "Being".*

Glossary

Conscious Use of Energy (CUE) – Directing the God energy or intention. CUE is a clue to us, to help us see what we're creating and the direction we're going with that creation.

Form/Body Energy - The uniqueness, the individualized essence created by God energy, Mind energy and Spirit energy. This is where souls pick the life they choose to live; their eye color, their hair color, weight, height, body shape and even their gender. If more Hue pours into Form, the body is more female. If more Pitch pours into Form, the body is more male. This place in Form is also the place of unique soul energy (USE).

Higher Master Self – The true spirit, without filters or human condition. It is the voice we hear from the heart.

Human Condition - Being unaware of our God power within. It is really all of the day-to-day human experience that we place more of a priority on than our own creative power and using God energy. We don't even know we're doing it. We're in the dark. They're old patterns of behavior that have become so much a part of us that we do it without thought. It's a reaction instead of a conscious choice.

Legwork – All those tangible things we do to create something. For example, if we desire a new job, legwork could include making a list of what the perfect job is for us, updating a resume, sending it out to potential employers, looking at want ads or working with a head hunter, putting the word out that we're looking for a new job, asking for the perfect job during meditation for our highest good and with great ease, etc.

Mind Energy – Pitch, Sound created by God energy. Pitch became the energy of Mind, which was the masculine side, the male energy. It is the speed of sound.

Mind's Choice – Everything we know from what we have been taught by our family of origin, religion, school, media, TV, etc. It creates our values and morals.

Non-Productive Emotion - Any emotion that does not aid us in our journey, such as people who are so depressed or angry, that they are not able to see clearly out of these emotions.

Productive Emotion – Any positive emotion or a negative emotion that is seen in a relatively quick time and the person is able to move through the issue and is able to use the emotion to help them find answers to their life.

Repressed – To exclude from consciousness such as traumatic events, abuse, etc. It's suppressing it so much we don't even remember it. They're stored in the etheric field.

Source/Infinite Energy- That energy that was void at first and at some point in the vastness of all things, creation became aware of Its own existence and it was Good. This is what we call God/Source/Infinite Energy which translates into God energy. Then this God energy reached out for more, not out of loneliness, but a desire to experience more in the vastness and so God made Spirit Energy (Hue or Light), Mind Energy (Pitch or Sound) and Form (Body) Energy.

Spirit Energy –Hue, Light created by God energy and this became the energy of Spirit. Hue is the feminine side, the female energy. It is also the speed of Light.

Spirit's Will – What our divine spirit knows is for our highest good and with great ease. Spirit's will communicates with us through the heart.

Suppressed - To consciously hold something down. We are aware of it, but don't want to deal with it. It is stored in the mind.

Suspended – Anything hanging around us in our mind and etheric field waiting to manifest at a time when conditions are perfect.

Unique Soul Energy (USE) - The essence and personality of who we are. This is also all the information from this lifetime and every past lifetime that this unique soul energy has experienced.

About the Author

Lynn Young is the daughter, granddaughter, and great-granddaughter of highly intuitive women. She is a wise and insightful mystic noted for her incredibly accurate, in-depth readings. The information Lynn brings forward is from the Enlightened Masters and each individual's Master Higher Self, thus allowing people to get the information needed to move forward in their lives.

Several years ago, Lynn received a gift from the universe: She became a full-body channel for "G". As a full body channel, she is completely disconnected from her body while "G" is present, removing her life 'filters' from what "G" says, thereby ensuring the purity of the information given. Because we live in a world of duality, "G" appears as male energy to balance the feminine energy of Lynn. However, in reality, "G" is androgynous.

"G" is an omniscient being of Divine Light who has come here to reawaken the knowledge of how to walk the master path that we have hidden from ourselves for thousands and thousands of years. He lovingly coaches us to help us uncover the God-like power we have forgotten so we can live highly effective, successful, and joyous lives. "G's" warm and loving presence, as well as his gentleness, wisdom, and wit, endear him to those who meet him. He is a dynamic, eloquent Spirit whose use of storytelling, diagrams and interactive discussions with the audience teach people how to live life in unconditional love and harmony.

Lynn's transformational company, Master Path LLC, sponsors seminars, workshops and classes that teach people how to transcend the human condition, shed the religious matrix and reclaim the spiritual life that is our birthright. The foundation of this knowledge is the Enlightened Principles revealed by "G". These principles help people to utilize and master the divine power within.

Lynn is an ordained minister with degrees in Communications and Art. She speaks at conferences and retreats for those who are on the road of enlightenment or those desiring a motivational speaker. There is no doubt that she can capture your attention and hold it.

She has authored her first book, *Being* and currently lives in Minneapolis, MN. Plans are in the works for many other books to follow.

Lynn can be reached through Master Path at 612-735-1540 or through the Master Path website, www.mastherpaths.com

Coming in Spring of 2007

MINNESOTA & 6TH

Jonathan Talbot was angry. Losing his sight due to a freak accident caused him to lose everything that he felt was important in life: the perfect woman, perfect job, and perfect friends. What he discovered was that the accident proved to him that the safe little world he thought he had created wasn't really safe after all. It fell apart, leaving him alone.

In a strange series of events, Jonathan finds himself sitting on a bench on the corner of Minnesota & 6th waiting for the bus. It is through this experience that he discovers the colorful characters of his life.

Yet there's one that seems to stand out from the rest. An interesting feeling comes over him whenever this particular person shows up to sit on the bus bench with him. The journey began with two simple words – "Good morning."

Jonathan learned through many conversations with the man how to be fearless, how to trust and reclaim what life he had left and how to change bitterness to sweetness. He also taught Jonathan how to find real love where he believed there was none.

It wasn't until a couple of years later, after the man had finished what he came to do and left, did Jonathan begin to realize that the man had been God himself!

Additional copies of "BEING" may be ordered from:

Master Path Publishing
701 Oak Park Lane, #92,
Hopkins, MN 55343
(952) 465-8034